Healing Stings

Healing Stings

Collected Poems

Pepertua K. Nkamanyang Lola

SPEARS MEDIA PRESS

The Lock on My Lips (A Play), Langaa Research and Publishing CIG (Winner of the 2015 EKO Price Award for Emerging Anglophone Writers, Drama Category)

Rustles on Naked Trees (A Novel), L' Harmattan (2015)

SPEARS MEDIA PRESS

7830 W. Alameda Ave, Suite 103 Denver, CO 80226

Spears Media Press publishes under the auspices of the Spears Media Association.

The Press furthers the Association's mission by advancing knowledge in education, learning, entertainment and research.

First Published 2016 by Spears Media Press
www.spearsmedia.com
info@spearsmedia.com
Information on this title: www.spearsmedia.com/Healingstings

Ordering Information:
Special discounts are available on bulk purchases by corporations, associations, and others. For details, contact the publisher at any of the addresses above.

ISBN: 978-1-942876-14-4 (Paperback)

For
My beloved husband and soul mate, Achiri Clement Nkamanyang, for his love, concern and exceptional character;

&

Those who believe that unity in diversity is a rich recipe for peace and security, and a stronger oxygen for the nation's develoPMent.

Contents

Philosophical Musings

The fangs of verse are the herbs of society.

It is no longer books that have an assignment for us. It is both us and books that have an assignment for each other.

It is the cohesion of the banana trunk and its suckers that arms the family tree with the authority and status of a traditional constituency.

It is the communion of the sugar cane chest and its clustering suckers that weaves the family threads in to solid roots.

If you want to know how filth looks like, visit the heart of beauty, If you want to separate life from performance, wear rags.

PROLOGUE I

Until the Roaring Tides of Extinction of Standards Abate

From the unfolding scene
Of the death of standards,
Where morals are shrinking,
And where like cowering insects
Education lies in a state of coma,
And the pulse of Africa's heart beat
No longer pounds with the clock,
Because like pests that blight yam tubers
On which they are suckled, nestled and cradled,
We sap the nation's fertile veins,
And maul from fatty bones of maps the best marrow,
And leave the nation's gnarled intestines
And sagging breasts naked and barren;
My verses will plant an academic clinic
With the melodious clothes of its words.
My verses will construct a social clinic
With the raging herbs of its words,
Until the colossal treasures of the brain become healing herbs;

And until the call to build and tap from pure sources
Has made the mind its home;
For Mighty verse must pollinate and tame
For our future, must mighty verse plant,
Until from the lips of verse, toxic debris is recycled or banished;
To keep alive the nation's hope of sprouting, breeding, blooming and
propagating.

From the unfolding scene of the fury of savagery
Where whispers of winds are thunderous;
And where under the hovering frenzy of thirsty knives

We crouch in agony shivering like curls and clothes of trees,
And from our furrowed faces flow floods and waterfalls of hot tears;
My soul nourishing verses will perform a mental surgery,
With the sprouting rustles of its verse;
Still, my soul nursing stings of verse will continue to rage,
Until when things into shreds fall apart
With dialogue and mediation we repair and restore;
And until from the heart and soul of the land,
Global scorch is routed out like still birth from the womb.

For these eggs of verse to hatch the herbs of verse,
The eggs that will germinate and creep around and suckle;
For these soul nourishing seeds of verse
To stretch their lineage across the borders of verse,
And like pumpkin vines flower and twine and creep along,
For the descent of verse flourishes and spread into genres,
And breed many more species of cross-pollinated cultivated verses,
Whose melody will suckle dry and famished minds,
Until we are interested, informed and involved;
Until our nation remain the treasure shrine of unity in diversity;
And until when tempers threaten to erupt,
With dialogue and negotiation we darn and reinstate;
Tamers and reapers of verse must water the seeds of verse
Until the choruses of our rhythms and anthems yield to the call for
seed sowing.

For these herbs of verse to feed us with moral diet,
And in the second stanza of our history
Meld humanity in diversity like a bunch of bananas;
Or a millipede that moves with all its one thousand legs;
Or a bundle of broomsticks that knows no divorce
For unity in diversity is the oxygen of the nation's develoPMent
And a rich recipe for peace building and security;
Farmers and reapers of verse must water the seeds of verse,
Until the tides of extinction hunkers down and abates.

Go, go, go you undying seeds of verse,
And into ailing minds inject your healing herbs,
And into other literary genres,
Impregnate, pollinate and ship your fecund genes,
For thy vaccines are the sperms for the head and heart.

From the unfolding scene
Of the eruption of delinquency and radicalism,
Where morality lies in its death bed
And where like the farts from the anus of grimacing clouds,
Intolerance germinates like dark brown sheets of rain clouds,
And hatch hideous species of rumbling extractions,
Which hang heavy above quaking heads like scowling clouds;
My verses will construct a Social Surgery
Where choristers of divorce will undergo mental Surgery;
Still my verses will construct a Holy Shrine
Where burglars and kidnappers of the nation's peace and security; Will
receive baptism and thorough cleansing.

For these herbs of verse to cleanse our bodies and souls,
The herbs that can tame savage instincts
And vaccinate minds against contagious influence,
Until from Africa and other climates,
Toxic consciousness is excreted,
And from stanzas divisive tendencies are uprooted,
And from chapters pestilent verses are deported,
And from blood streams extreme passions are extradited,
And from young minds trappings of drug addiction are repatriated,
And from customs corrosive creeds are evacuated,
And from the Social Media venomous lures are eradicated;
And from agendas child-trafficking is banished,
And from classrooms cults are wrenched off,
And from society the reign of intolerance is nipped on the bud,
And from lips narratives of babies becoming mothers are history;

For only feelings of oneness must we plant and nurture;
Love, tolerance, patience and patriotism must we sow,
And our differences must we learn to mend,
With the threads and tissues of negotiation and dialogue.

Go, go, go you Mighty Pen, Head Lines, Theatre and Social Media and social preachers,
Go, go, go stage and tales and consumers of the arts;
Be not hawkers of grumbling and thundery situations;
Be not the hero whose relics are cripples and corpses;
Be not the mother whose breast-milk is toxic,
Be not the composite that kills the soils it fertilizes.
Still, be not sycophants or advocates of divorce.
Open the laps of verse
And from that vast highway of mental catchment,
Wherein is nestled well cradled future melodies,
And rustles and herbs of mighty pen;
Hatch planters, builders and proactive generations of social bees,
Whose melodious and raging anthems
Will fulfil moral and national duty,
And halt the fading wines of the purity of values,
For thy duty be to plant the future,
For thy duty be to hatch, suckle and tame,
And wean your branches off corrosive consciousness.

Abuja, May-June, 2016

PROLOGUE II

The Eggs of Verse

With the melody of verse,
The exploits of great hunters will I sing,
And like the trunk of a pregnant mountain,
Their works like history will be erected,
And the trails of their exploits enacted;
For the footprints of their harvests,
Are the spices of my lyrics.

With the fangs of my verse,
The flesh of stings and stinks will I sting,
And like an infected fetus in a butchered womb,
Their sick plans like a premature baby will be aborted;
For when the viper has hatched,
The viper and its hatchery must be eliminated,
For the wounds must be healed,
For the body to be restored;
And the herbs must be hatched
By the stings of soul nourishing verses,
And dig up pests by their roots.

Abuja, June, 2016

ACKNOWLEDGEMENT

My most-heartfelt gratitude goes to the following colleagues, reviewers, and sources/persons to whom I owe a special debt of gratitude: Charles Teke Ngiewe, the exceedingly proficient, versatile and fertile researcher in African Literature, and also Professor of English Literature who performed the arduous task of proof-reading, editing the poems and providing useful suggestions for improvement, which have been appreciatively incorporated into the individual poems. In addition, this collection has received comprehensive and insightful dimensions from Teke's very nutritive foreword that has in no small way opened up certain social and critical perspectives I never even contemplated at the time of foraging for mental diet. The story of my arduous creative expedition would be partially told if I fail to mention that the poems also benefited immensely from Nforbin Gerald's resourcefulness in linguistic and context-sensitive issues which were all very vital in shaping the content of certain poems. The insightful endorsements from inspired luminaries like Lem Lilian Atanga, Kevin Ngo Toh and Peter Suh-Nfor Tangyie cannot go unnoticed. My kids; Nkamanyang Grodjinovski Fombu Junior and Nkamanyang Maclouski Ngambam furnished me with insightful indigenous tales they learned during their short stay in the village with grandparents. The contributions mentioned above broadened my thinking and only go to confirm schools of thought that perceive the entire production of a work of art as incomplete without external critical opinion. I do savour the rewrite more than the writing itself. Any unnoticed weaknesses are exclusively my responsibility.

PREFACE

It is no longer books that have an assignment for writers. It is both books and writers that have assignments for each other. There is a disproportionately creative and attendant critical void, although gradually being filled, in the discipline of Anglophone poetry, in Cameroon. My experience of supervising students end-of year dissertations, and teaching poetry to students at the Secondary School (on part-time basis and freelance), and particularly the undergraduate and Postgraduate levels of education in Cameroon Universities has left me with the impression that a majority of students hardly display sufficient mastery of the generic features of poetry, as well as the criteria that can be useful for differentiating poetry from other literary genres. Questions relating to the structure of poetry (metre, rhythm, feet and stanzas), phonological structures (rhymes and other sound forms), morphological and syntactic structures (word repetition and poetic syntax) as well as semantic structures (imagery) are hardly distinguished from each other with accurate determining poetic strategies. In addition, the question of how poetic devices such as moods, senses, sounds, experience, feelings, emotions, impressions, rhythm, self-reflexivity, perspective, desires and subjectivity (which are amongst the excavation sites of poetry) are constructed is hardly satisfactorily answered. Last but not the least, questions about metre, rhythm, feet, poetic functions of language and the attitude of the poet towards subject matter and target audience are most often inadequately addressed. Lack of generic variety appears to slow down research in African/Cameroon Anglophone Poetry, hence, there is relative absence in the English Departments of Cameroon Universities, of dissertations whose conceptual, descriptive and analytical frameworks are specifically poetic theories. In other words, a majority of dissertations on poetry investigate thematic issues, although it is most often form and structures that open the interpretive door to themes.

There has been few fruitful attempts from Cameroonian critics however, to suggest some criteria that can be useful, as distinguishing and theoretical guides, for poetry interpretation and analysis. Ground breaking as they are, many of such attempts suggest theoretical criteria for analysing issues relating to semantic, morphological and syntactic structures thereby ignoring other poetic patterns that require criteria for interpretation far beyond linguistic devices. Although Peter Suh-NforTangie's and Edward Muwah Cheng's scintillating *Prose and Poetry Appreciation Handbook* (2008) provides lovers of Cameroon poetry with a catalogue of rudiments that may distinguish a piece of text as a poem as well as serve as interpretive criteria for poetry analysis, this attempt, like Nkengasong's illuminating 'Stylistic Approach" remains less exploited by students writing their dissertations in poetry. Further, the rich repertoires of poetry collections produced by Cameroon colossuses of English expression such as Bernard Fonlon, Bate Besong, Nkemngong Nkengasong, Nol Alembong, Mathew Takwi, and Shadrack Ambanasom amongst others, and for which the differentiating, definable and interpretive services of theoretical attempts can be solicited, are not readily accessible to the Cameroonian student specializing in poetry, and have thus been less exploited in dissertations which tend to show a tendency towards analysis of themes and social issues, thereby privileging for analysis, the historical and the sociological, and thus ignoring genres and poetic structures.

Besides the relative absence of poetry collections and dissertations in English/African Literature Departments in Cameroonian Universities focusing their analysis on the purely generic features of poetry, most existing collection of poems reveal a tendency towards certain genres and themes. The relative scarcity of poetry collections that pay a copious attention to the syntactic, phonological, morphological and semantic structures could imply that critical/interpretive endeavours focusing their analysis on the structures of poetry might be uncommon. This could partly explain why Cameroonian students using poetic material as data for their dissertations are yet to have need for the Stylistic Approach developed by Nkengasong, the Post-Modern hybrid genre theory of poetry developed by Pilar Abad Garcia (2005), the

Transgeneric narratological poetic theory developed by Peter Huhns (2004), as well as the more sophisticated 'multi-component model' developed by Eva Muller-Zettlemann (2000) which brings together a range of criteria for systematizing and defining poetry in the form of analytical strategies.

The consequences of the scarcity and or tendency of some poetry collections towards certain poetic types/genres is that Cameroonian students writing dissertations in poetry have often used the insights of New Historicism, Socio-logical Criticism, Marxism, Postcolonial theories, Feminist and Gender frameworks amongst others for analytical purposes. Such theories are context-sensitive and would inevitably prove deficient in locating the generic, structural and semantic complexities that differentiate between the various poetic forms on the one and between poetry and other literary genres on the other. The result of importing theoretical frameworks from Historical contexts (Sociological and Marxist approaches, Feminist approaches, New Historicism), Author-oriented approaches (Biographical approaches and Psychoanalytical approaches), Gender studies, Postcolonial Criticism, and influence studies, and forcing them where they may not exhaustively apply is that most dissertations analysing Cameroon/African poetry often privilege contexts such as history, sociocultural, ideological, and political issues as suitable subjects for poetry, hence revealing a sheer neglect of the generic features that typify poetry as a genre in its own right.

If lack of exposure either to a diversity of poetic types, or theories of poetry, as the case may seem, could be the reasons why dissertations on poetry, produced by students in Cameroon Universities often ignore both the generic/distinguishing traits of poetry and the theoretical frameworks for poetry analysis, and rather focus largely on author oriented and context-sensitive issues, then, there is enough reasons for writers of poetry to consider stretching the scope of the less tapped poetic types and patterns of poetic genres as well as pay more attention to further levels of structural, phonological, syntactic, paradigmatic, and semantic complexities largely ignored in dissertations and some collections of poems. Issues relating to musicality and lyricism, subjectivity, lines, metric and stanzaic structure, perspective, rhythm, feet, rhymes, sound patterns, word repetition, poetic syntax, and imagery deserve further attention than we have attributed to them. I do not pretend to have filled the gaps identified above in my own collection. The present volume is however an attempt to address some of the deficits that are usually very manifest during classroom interactions and in my supervision or reading of dissertations focusing on poetry analysis.

The main objective of this volume, although not limited to, is to:

1. Write poetry that is responsive to the needs of pedagogy and language that uses as vehicles of expression mental pictures as well as the rage, rustles, murmurs, whispers, sounds and sighs of words;

2. Provide different kinds of poems whose anthropological residues, objects, generic features, structures (meter, rhythm, feet, stanzas), phonological (rhymes and sound patterns), morphological and syntactic structures, and most importantly semantic structures (imagery) can stretch the arsenal of linguistic, mental and environmental (ecological) imagery which can determine the selection/choice of analytical framework, and open up innovative areas of interest for the interpretation and analysis of Cameroon/African poetry in particular and poetry in general;

3. Create an academic maternity whose brain children are feelings, emotions, subjectivity, moods, attitudes, and states of mind in general.

4. Create grounds for seeing poetry itself as a Social Welfare Centre or Social Clinic, a teacher, healer, advocate and moralist;

5. Draw attention to the need to write poetry garnish with fecund and distilled imagery, and characterized for the most part, by a spurt of moods, emotions and feelings whose mental pictures can constitute the key to the vast environmental and social pressures that post-independent global societies usually do not escape.

I am not quite sure I met the target goals. Nonetheless, if the language of feelings, emotions, moods and mental pictures should sting and heal the same way herbs do; or speak, bark and rage in place of machine guns, bombs, missiles and bullets, one important thing will happen: poetic discourse will blossom and germinate with 'translinguistic' and modified species of functions, mental herbs, imagery, and linguistic structures which, will in turn replace savagery, violence, bombs, traps, and guns which have no other function than unleash toxic consciousness, death, and anarchy into the world. When that happens, the goal of poets will stretch beyond being just 'social commentators', to that of pedagogues and social herbalists. In this regard I hope, these verses will reinforce P. B. Shirley's implicit articulation of the need to use poetry as a herbal tool when he said poets are the unacknowledged legislators of the world. If my poetry should dress like a herbalist and assume the role of healing the gaping moral potholes on the walls of our deeds and intensions, the world could become a better place to live in.

Born of both the stings and herbs of verse; the moods, emotions, feelings, thoughts, rhythms, taste, and states of mind are the fuels and vehicles from which the subjective and innermost processes of the suburbs of the soul and brain are hatched and which in turn contribute to recreate the very unmediated flow of feelings and mental processes that gave birth to the children of verse. Subjectivity, narrative lyrics hardly uncontaminated of story-telling emphasis, experience, feelings, and impressions are some of the vehicles through which the multifaceted social issues of gender, politics, identity, colonial/national history, savagery, good governance, patriotism, national integration, peace building, conflict and conflict resolution strategies, security, tolerance, corruption, disease and death, the need for a reinforced culture of maintenance, morality and ethics, nature, etc. are born. It is thus hoped that the generic and social content of these young verses which, in different degrees of emphasis include lyrics, narrative verses, verse drama, meaningful objects, folk culture, body metaphors, semantic, phonological, syntactic and structural complexities, etc., will bring to scholars and students of Cameroon/African poetry modified genres of poetry and species of creativity.

Perpetua K. Nkamanyang Lola.

FOREWORD

Pepertua Lola's *Healing Stings*, comprising forty-one superbly crafted poems, is an undeniable advancement in artistic creativity and positions her as a poet engaged with multifaceted aspects of human existence and experience. This collection is a laudable contribution to the literary mine known as Cameroon Anglophone literature which is presently attracting national, continental and global attention. Both the aesthetic and thematic perspectives of the poems lend credence to a mind which not only masters poetic register but also a deep sense of human value. The collection engages questions on relevant contemporary issues such as gender, social malaise, eco-consciousness, politics, peace, and conflict resolution.

Lola provides her collection with two very absorbing prologues which herald her collection's preoccupations. Prologue 1 and Prologue 2 are respectively entitled 'Until the Roaring Tides of Extinction of Standards Abate' and 'The Eggs of Verse'. They express with finesse Lola's diagnoses of social malaise and healing measures through the might of the pen. The following lines of the first poem capture this unwavering concern:

From the unfolding scene
Of the death of standards,
Where morals are shrinking,
And where like cowering insects
Education lies in a state of coma...
My verses will plant an academic clinic
With the melodious clothes of its words;
My verses will construct a social clinic
With the raging herbs of its words,
My verses will construct a mental Surgery...

'The Eggs of Verse' takes the cue by reiterating Lola's determination:
With the melody of verse,
The exploits of great hunters will I sing,
And like the trunk of a pregnant mountain,
Their works like history will be erected,
And the trails of their exploits enacted;
For the footprints of their harvests,
Are the spices of my song.

With the fangs of my verse,
The flesh of stings and stinks will I sting,
And like an infected foetus in a butchered womb,
Their sick plans like a premature baby will be aborted;
For when the viper has hatched,
The viper and its hatchery must be eliminated,
For the wounds must be healed,
For the body to be restored;
And the herbs must be hatched
By the stings of these verses.

With such refined determination, Lola can sail her reader through a series of breath-taking poems in which *Healing Stings* reverberate.

Poems on Gender persist on the epistemology of re-imaging and re-imagining gender, bordering on masculinity and femininity, on the deconstruction and reconstruction of gender stereotypes and biases, and most especially on the bonding of both female and male in cultural and social ordering. In this section which I consider the fundamental pillar of the collection, Lola displays a vibrant sense of cultural consciousness and intelligence regarding power dynamics of gender. Her intellectual background has sharpened her sense of value judgement on the subject of the sensitive issues of patriarchy and the woman's position within structures of power.

I choose to analyse Lola from a postcolonial paradigmatic perspective without losing sight of the fact that her collection can be subject to any other theoretical precepts. Postcolonial criticism provides a genuine local and global dimension of construing and interpreting her textualisation of the human predicament. The strength of the poet's cultural reasoning and intelligence is enshrined in her womanist, stiwanist and negro-feminist inclinations to draw from the criticism of Afro-feminist scholars such as Molara Ogundipe-Leslie and Obioma Nnaemeka. The woman in the cultural ordering of mothering is one of Lola's central pre-occupation in this section as well. She resoundingly captures the anatomy of female power in social and cultural processes which usually consciously or unconsciously debases or puts the woman at the margins in such processes. This supposed underprivileged situation ignites agency in the woman which is vital in transformational dynamics.

In celebrating the woman, Lola in 'Domestic Luminaries II' concentrates on mothering which is one of the most central issues in the African woman's mind-set. Culturally, to have a child or children is sign of fertility and re-productiveness and a consolidation of the woman's place in society. From a philosophical perspective the absence of a child or sense of mothering causes existential anguish and uncertainty.

Another important ingrained typology or semantic field of mothering which Lola images is that which goes beyond procreation; it is the commitment of mothers to nurture and raise their child/ren to become successful. Catherine Acholonu, in *Motherism: The Afrocentric Alternative to Feminism* (1995) distinguishes between African feminisms and EuroAmerican feminisms in terms of mothering which to her constitutes the core of African female thinking. In "Motherhood in African Literature and Culture" (2011) Remi Akujobi has rightly underscored the semantic shifts in questions bordering on motherhood. He asserts that:

> In many societies, motherhood is wrapped in many cultural and religious meanings - cultural as in what the society thinks a mother should be, that is, some elements associated with a mother, and religiously, in what the practiced faith of a particular society attaches to motherhood. Motherhood assumes different names and shapes depending on the society that is

practicing it. The word procreation or giving birth and nurtur-
ing new life whether physically or otherwise has led to different
definitions of the words "feminine," "maternal," and "feminine
spirituality" in many cultures and religious traditions. Mother-
hood in some quarters is seen as a sacred and powerful spiritual
path for a woman to take. In literature and in other discourses
alike, motherhood is a recurrent theme across cultures. It is one
striking term in women's discourse that is given prominence.
Motherhood has been viewed by many in different lights and
presented in diverse ways. Motherhood as an experience and as
an institution has and is still receiving different definitions from
different writers both men and women today. (2)

Akujobi's articulation is very central in understanding the cultural
matrices from which Lola positions discourses on mothering and wom-
anhood. While she may be inclined to her own cultural epistemology of
mothering or maternal consciousness, her poems point to the semantic
plurality of this category in a global context.

In the poem 'The Language of Breasts and Beards', Lola ascertains
her status as advocate of the woman, basing her arguments on grounds
of mutual inclusivity. The poem's imagery is very rich and conveys a
strong sense of reciprocity between men and women. Lola's feminist
poetics and politics indicate that the woman's strategic signpost should
be lodged in the centre of the man who cannot extricate himself from
her. In this vein, the man valorises the woman and gives her due worth
and recognition.

'No Longer on Stage' questions man as stage director and the place
of the woman as culturally bound to perform assigned roles as if she
is merely mimicking and enacting theatrical performances. Otherwise
said, the poet militates for the re-positioning of the woman in her
natural and dynamic role as agent of develoPMent and worthwhile
cultural life, subtly appealing for man to empower the woman rather
than devising means of disempowering her with a mind and voice
which are naturally not hers:

Welcome to the dining table;
Thinking together and sowing together,
For the future must we together plant,
Welcome to the dining table,
For access and awareness must we,
In the same measure embrace.

This poem therefore echoes the above mentioned, 'The Language of Breasts and Beards', underlining Lola's advocacy for men to acknowledge the natural potentials and endowments of the woman. This would dismantle male exclusionary attitude and bring the woman on board for mutual consent and betterment of society.

'The Journey' captures the revolutionary and evolutionary nature of the woman. The poem finely images the woman as an agent of mutation and transformation inscribed in the poet's call for her to go beyond any culturally or socially imposed boundaries:

From now on women from weavers to builders become,
From now on the margins from menders to makers become,
From now on the colony within, from silence to architects become,
From now on the masses from messengers to managers become,
From now on the half-baked from consumers to inventors become,
From now on learners from harvesters to authors become,
From now on commentators from critics to writers become,
From now on women from cleaners to constructors become,
From now on women from child-bearers to creators become,
And henceforth the hands from labour to manufacturers become.

Salient questions remain to be answered regarding this poem: What class of woman is Lola actually concerned with in such contemporary times? Rural? Urban? To attempt these questions would largely depend on the paradigmatic stance of the critic on Lola, but it is certain that she views the woman from myriad locations and sensibilities.

"Poems on Social Ills, Ethics and Religious Morality" portray the poet as social legislator who expresses contemptuousness regarding degrading societal values and practices. This section, otherwise said, showcases Lola's imaginative maturity as she explicitly textualises salient social problems evolving around ethics and spiritual sterility. 'Judgement Day' is a long poem with a prophetic warning which Lola uncompromisingly directs to those who spend their time robbing the country of its resources for selfish and under-develoPMental ends. Some of the poem's excerpts are worth commenting on:

When at the threshold of Judgement Day,
Like a slaughter house your report card will be bleeding,
And from the womb of your report card
A continuous streaming of premenstrual menstruation,
Because extra-large pregnant pockets with financial obesity afflicted,
Because your financial hive from financial constipation blighted,
Because your financial garner stashed in foreign soils excavated.
While awaiting deportation order and appropriate action;
Your clock from cardiac arrest will suffer,
While your heart like tremors will tremble,
Invading your ears like roaring earthquakes,
Annexing your ears like the sound of pounding hooves.

When at the threshold of Judgement Day,
The gates of Kondengui flung open its fangs;
Ready to swallow small and big fishes;
Ready to consume midges and elephants,
Ready to strangle architects and swindlers,
Ready to expose arbitrators and adjudicators,
Ready to unearth hawkers of marks and endangered species,
For morals are in danger of erosion,
And values in danger of corrosion;
Legal daggers will rage above heads,
To stem the tides of moral extinction.

When at the threshold of Judgement Day,
The Legal Dagger will mount the throne of Judgment,

And in a thunderous tone declares a death penalty;
Like a mountain humbled by an eruption,
Your pride will begin to blink and shrink,
Like epileptic heartbeats of quaking mountains.
And still like a blank and naked map,
Your page will look like a bare and barren reign
And like a debtor hiding from creditors,
The door of your stomach will be shot even at lunchtime.

These lines evince a conviction that a country is drained of its financial potentials, and there certainly will be a time for reckoning for those involved in such malpractices. Lola forestalls the bleakness which awaits perpetrators of economic and financial asphyxiation. Embezzlement and gross mismanagement of public funds are a serious postcolonial malaise which has led to untold hardship and poverty for those who are not in the position to unlawfully appropriate for themselves. The imagery is enriching; "your report card will be bleeding", "extra-large pregnant pockets with financial obesity", "financial hive", "your heart like tremors will tremble", "gates of Kondengui flung open its fangs" "legal Dagger" and "epileptic heartbeats of quaking mountains", all point to the stark reality which characterizes economic mismanagement and its attending consequences. The significance of *Healing Stings* in this context would be seen in the financial alleviation of the poor and dispossessed which the sledge hammer of justice would ignite.

This poem shares affinities with 'Bleeding the Heart of Africa Dry' which in metaphorical terms superbly delineates a society that is reduced to the commodification of services and void of any ethical values related to monetary transaction:

The race for "Gombo" is in its full gear.
In the silent hours of the dark tappers lurk around
Along the corridors of juicy habitats they crawl in suits;
Milking nations and draining Anthems,

Extracting the nutrients which feed the nation's blood streams,
Draining the energy which feeds the pores on the skin of Anthems.
Payrolls infested with Ghost-workers,
Payrolls flooding with Bush Fallers,
Payrolls inundated with corpses,
Because the race for "Gombo" is in its full gear.

Because the race for "Gombo" is in its full gear,
The once overflowing river now shrivelling and shrinking
And the ribs and bones on the chests of nations are exposed;
The once brimming breasts on the chests of Anthems
Are dehydrating and withering,
The once spilling over fountain now leaking
And the lungs of nations are dry and thirsty;
The once fecund womb of Africa now barren
The lungs of states are perforated;
The blood streams of nations fast dehydrating and desiccating,
The pillars on which we lean withering, shrivelling, and shrinking
The legs on which we walk limping and staggering
The sap that feeds our stomachs bleeding dry,
For the juice on which we suckle is draining.
Like brim-full streams and lakes withering because of climate change,
The baobab may one day shrink in breath and body build.
And when the pores on Africa's skin are blinking,
For multiple salary codes were shouldered by one person
Complicity, collusion and venality,
The holes through which State coffers are sapped,
And now poverty announces itself,
Despite efforts from Government to strangle corruption.

A majority of Cameroonians are familiar with the coinage "Gombo" which connotes bribery and corruption in the execution of both government and private services. Bad governance and the annihilation of good practices have taken precedence over attitudes which foster growth and develoPMent. Lola presents this cankerworm of systematic corruption which has deflated the nation and literarily squeezed out its life. Draining, withering, shrivelling, bleeding, shrinking, dehydrating, Desiccating, limping and staggering are imagistic in portraying a disembodied nation at the verge of complete collapse.

'Vaccinate the Judiciary', 'Vaccinate the Continent' and 'Social Menu' are among the poems in which the poet prescribes a therapy to the socioeconomic and political pathologies which the nation and continent face. In the poems Lola's clarion call is the purgation of deterrents of justice and continental growth and sustainability. In her context, vaccinating would mean both a preventive and curative measure.

'At the Tribunal of Ethics and Conscience' is an elevated dramatic piece and prosaic in nature which grapples with another dimension in Lola's social engagement. The text is very rich in didactic quality and captures psycho-philosophical trends which according to the poet hamper moral and spiritual uprightness. Lola uses allegory in staging a trial involving God, Man of God, Society and Western historical figures such as Nietzsche, Marx, Feuerbach, Machiavelli, Freud and Sartre, who immensely influenced philosophical and religious thought in the nineteenth and twentieth centuries. These personalities challenged Judeo-Christian assumptions and dogmas, advocating atheist poetics and eliciting a global impact from which Lola's society cannot extricate itself. In the text they are indicted for their controversies and sentenced to change their tone so as not to infringe on Christian tenets which are necessary to avert the calamity in which the world finds itself. There is clear indication that Lola's Christian inclination is pitted against the supposed excesses of these seminal thinkers. The poem most importantly gives room for diverse critical opinions.

It is very interesting to note that Lola's advocacy for Christian tenets in assuaging social degradation does not presuppose the commodification of Christianity. In the poem entitled 'Religious Democracy', drawn from the section which is centred on politics and history, she bitterly decries the proliferation of churches which seem to have lost sight of genuine Christian values:

Religious democracy breeds prostitution

Its drainages floods with migrants, immigrants and nomads.
Because non-achievers and Ex-convicts are proprietors of churches;
While their wives and children are church Accountants and Bankers.
While for the proprietors of these commercial enterprises
Evangelization is less traumatic and juicy business
For conscience and moral law, the sheep is fed with filth.

Kitchens and bedrooms host churches;
Like commercial enterprises churches swell with contractors, While
the Gospel is advertised, commercialized and sold
And Holy creeds marketed, wholesaled, and retailed
Sacraments are hawked, traded and vended;
And like Sexually Transmissible Marks
Miracles are drainage strategies.

This poem indicates that Christianity should neither be taken for
a joke nor contextualized in a capitalist culture.

Lola is already known as a crusader of eco-consciousness and
environmental sustainability and a convinced champion of postcolonial
green thinking. "Nature and Environmental Poetry" fosters her com-
mitment to postcolonial ecologies. 'Roars and Swooshes of Menchum
Falls' is an extensive poem which underscores a series of ecological
concerns. Some excerpts are worth citing:

Thou cradle of Africa's wealth,
Your beauty consumes my soul,
The breeze that kisses my cheeks,
And lures eyes to sleep while the mind is roused;
And like the inspired mind
Eager to forage for mental food;
A wealth of imaginative possibilities evoked.

Your veins with lavish nutrients vibrate,
The vessels of your womb with fats and fuel erupted.
Like fresh palm wine dripping into a calabash,

Your nutritive womb with milk overflows.
Like fecund flow from maternal habitat
Your muscular branches with gas and oil floods,
The fuel of Cameroon's millennium hope,
Reminiscent of your potency and virility;
For according to the dream,
When thy laps menstruate, Africa is alive.

These lines convey the immense potentials which this indescrib-able scenario possesses. The imagery invokes the Romantic tradition enshrined in Shelley and Wordsworth, though having a localised speci-ficity with regard to economic potentials.

From an eco-cultural perspective the twin Falls and environment are not just natural phenomena without ingrained cultural patterning. Their exoteric and transcendental proportions point to the inextrica-ble attachment which man has with them. Lola therefore signals an extension to Western powered notions of eco-criticism by bringing in experiences which are culturally specific to African ecological thinking:

O Menchum Twin Falls, the hope of Africa,
The fecund and untainted abode of the divinities,
The sacred and untainted dwelling of immortals,
Like the waterfall of menses from your weeping laps,
Your nutrients and diving waters are lures for tourists and investors.
Corrosive pipes burrow through and rape your virgin laps,
And tap from its well cradled breasts all the juicy marrow;
When your womb will shrink and shrivel;
And the milk in the breast of your soil
Wrenched off like unwanted weeds;
When you are no more,
Africa and her groom will mourn more and more.

No one would doubt that Lola is desirous to have the Menchum Falls remain in their natural state without any human incursion, given their sacredness. The envisaged human activity to be carried out on this site would obviously deteriorate the naturalness of the falls. This explains why Lola goes further to subtly caution against any human attempt at distorting the uniqueness of the falls and their environs.

With regard to literary historicity Lola's recourse to history cannot be overemphasised. History provides useful material which the poet manipulates with artistic acuity to pass on her message. 'The Raging 90s' underlines the bleak and tumultuous phase of Cameroon's history in the 1990s. The country was caught in a kind of deterministic wind of change from which it emerged fragile but not docile. Lola here shows the intersection between memory and nation, history and change, and literature and narrating the nation.

Lola's sensitivity to peace and nation building is worthy of praise. In an era of insurgency and threats on a global scale, national peace and security are deemed as vitally primordial to the poet. Poems like 'The Wedding', 'Defend the Flag' and 'Cameroon' hinge on a strong sense of nationalism and promotion of unity and integrity. 'The Wedding' is an apt expression of Cameroon's transcolonial history which uniquely left her entangled in a dual colonial legacy (French and British) from which she should profit. The same logic is pursued in 'Defend the Flag'.

'Where the Pen Rules' is a powerful poem which images the extraordinary power of the writer in social and political conditioning. Through the power of their pen, the writer is an uncontested agent of alternation and transformation in most postcolonial states. Lola's poem therefore reminds one of the pen as barrel in Ngugi wa Thinog'o's *Penpoints, Gunpoints, and Dreams*. Cultural nationalism is another dimension where the poet displaces the power of the pen. This is evinced in the poem 'The Plaited-Ropes' in which African writers are urged to use all cultural resources at their disposal to enrich their artistic potentials for the world to know and recognise the continent's importance in the global market of cultures. Lola may be concerned with her motherland Cameroon, but by extension Africa and the world for genuine postcolonial globalization. While the writer's aim is primarily to impact society, there is no doubt that society also has to recognise their effort. The poem 'Where the Pen Heals' moves in this direction. The reader is left to savour its contents.

This foreword is not an attempt at orienting the reader on any interpretative measure in Lola's poetry. It cannot do critical justice to the entire collection. It is simply an intellectual invitation to explore the richness and depth of the collection, because a few comments would not serve as the appropriate portal to this very distinctive bulk of poetic grandeur. Healing Stings as the title of the collection carries with it, is an important metaphorical marker. Stings which heal indicate Lola's commitment in exposing and redressing gender, social, political and environmental problems. I hereby strongly acknowledge her as a legislator particularly for the timeliness of the work. Lola has not only exposes these problems, she suggests the need to redress them with insight and subtlety. She is unequivocal in her contemptuousness, unflinching in her indictment, but very rational and human in her prescribed remedy. Her communicative potentials evince mastery of the English language. Here lies her genius and force in strengthening and straightening human values. The power of the poet is the word; the word of the poet is an elicitor to action. Healing Stings brilliantly showcases Lola's mettle in this perspective. She deserves a due place not only in the pantheon of Cameroon female Anglophone writers, but also Cameroon literature as a broad category.

June 2016

-Charles Ngiewih Teke

Poems on Gender

2

Domestic Luminaries I (For Mary)

Her laps were my nest
Nipples in my Lips
Drizzle like rain drops
And chilled like fruit juice.

On her back I straddled
Her arms were my nest
Lullabies she did sing
And my bedtime balm.

The hatchery she hatched
Territory of her womb
Germinating like sprouts
Banana trunk and suckers.

With seeds her womb sprouts
Like leaves your home blooms
And teems just like shoots
In your domestic hive

The seeds of her womb
Darted from her laps
Swarming like locusts
In her hatchery.

Every Mondays Tuesdays,
Popping out from her loins
Producing he-goats
The most cherished seeds.

Every Wednesdays Thursdays
Bursting with suckers
Triplets and twin births
Just like traffic flow,
From Fridays, Saturdays
Her home like a bee hive,
Looks like clothes of trees,
Fresh like pumpkin leaves.

Like the shepherd and flock
Bearded stories were told,
The bat and the sun,
And the wicked witch.

My stockings she stitched
For the needle her school
My hair that she braids
Flushing like green curls.

The quarrels she mends
Surges she subdued
The tempests she tamed
Peace the mighty price.

The growls that she pruned
The rumbles she tamed
The eruptions unleashed
With lullabies she quenched.

Fireside stories we sang,
The house-wife was the witch,
The farm lands she farmed
At night she garnered.

The tortoise, the pig,

4

Grinding stone and its scabbard,
Was the archive she mined,
From the bearded tale.

The hands that you chained
In the fence were confined
The hands you tethered
To pound with pestles.

The ghetto you carved
The cage was her home,
The world you landscaped
Your song she did sing.

The fruits of their wombs
Her love on all poured,
And the mouths that she fed
She was like foliage.

The song that we sing
Awareness we want
Equality we seek
And empowerment.

With voice we have carved,
The song that we sing,
The drum that we beat
The storm is abating.

Say no to the lock
With which lips were locked
Say no to the rope
On her tethered hands.

The Birth of Voice

From the hatchery of the shadows emerge,
From the maternity of the shadows spring up,
Like mushrooms sprout and wear the crown,
In ravishing curls flourish like the hair of corn,
And from the cultural cage,
Shade off the cocoon;
And like pupa from the shell
From the incubator emerge.

From the bosom of the ghetto,
Where the cultural birth certificate claims,
Was your place of birth and growth;
Spring up like mushrooms,
And like a foetus in the womb,
Dart out like a new birth,
And from the incubator emerge.

From the cocoon to butterfly
No longer in the hatchery
Waiting to be programmed
No longer in the dominion
Waiting to be sectioned up.

Break the calabash though the surface may be slippery;
And from that prison must the foetus be born;
From creeping and staggering to leaping and mountaineering,
Look no more to woman as the target and beneficiary,
Let not breast and curves and menses determine my performance,
With a cluster of hands plant we two and water,
And climb the ladder of liberty to the summit,
For the house must be built with all the four hands.

On the steering wheel of develoPMent,
Must we two sit firm and drive along, for
It is no longer man that has an assignment for woman,
It is no longer man that has questions and answers for woman,
It is man and woman that have assignments for each other.

Domestic Luminaries II

Tethered hands held my hands
Deep cuts in her palms
The blisters bleeding
Like a butcher's slab.

Furrowed hands nuzzle my hands
And tend them and tamed
She grafted and pruned
Today I blossomed.

Punctured palms pricked my hands
Potholes in her palms
My tummy she fed
Today I grow round.

Craggy hands gripped that hoe
Over furrows she hunched
The seeds she nurtured
Hunger she conquered.

Over ridges she hunched
Digging till nightfall,
And the harvest garnered
My school needs she raised.

Thorny hands held my hands
Bringing joy and hope
Abandoned souls she reared
No pay, no fanfare.

The smile on my face,
The joy in your home,
Blooming out like blooms,
Is her mighty price
And her salary, salary, salary. (2x)

Section Me Up: The Colony Within

The land to man was allocated
The crops to woman were allotted,
The trunk with man was associated
The branch with woman was equated,
The foliage with man was related
The roots with woman were connected.

Her hibernation they programed,
Her destination decided,
Her frustration facilitated,
Her choices determined,
Her program drafted and dictated,
Her salary in teaspoon measured,
Yet her ambition resurrected.

Her Joys fragmented,
Her hopes amputated,
Her happiness fractured,
Her future ruptured,
And claim the colony within
Which they carved with the Queen's melodious linguistics
And threatening indigenous vocabulary,
Which threatens trespassers with persecution;
Was like barren soil,
Just like mental dwarfs,
With which she was compared
Were like stagnant waters.
In stigma she was soaked,
But their tempest she roused,
Just because she did dream,
And to Beijing she stormed

To diagnose and heal.

At the rear she perched,
Yet, from page to page she foraged for food,
For mental menu she rummaged and hunted,
And the mental diet she foraged,
In dozes she was served.

The fibre from palm fronds she extracted,
Like minerals she excavated,
Like palm wine she tapped,
Like an addict she was drugged,
Like a scavenger she scavenged,
And as the mental menu
Was devoured with greed,
With ink she conquered
With voice she claimed
With a dose, she was healed.

When like a born-again she floated up
And mounted the stage,
The mountain was erected
To raise an objection.
Like the judge, he thundered:
"Subjection my love"!
Like a cajoling lawyer she muffled a rustle:
"Objection my Lord."

The Language of Breasts and Beards

It doesn't matter
Whether beards, whether breasts
Equality we seek
Equal access for all.

It doesn't matter
Whether trousers, whether skirts
Liberation we seek
Equal access for all.

It doesn't matter
Whether office, whether home
The tempests abating
Boundaries are banished.

It doesn't matter
Whether cripples, whether dwarfs
The whirlwind waning
Mountains are dwindling.

It doesn't matter
Whether hills or foothills
The barb wires battered
Our share is assured.

If to carvers, voice belongs to man while nod to woman belongs,
Our melded voice reaps its strength from being garrulous.
The seas are now calm
Caged voices sour high.

It doesn't matter
Whether standing or squatting
On the decision table
Her voice is now heard.

It doesn't matter
Whether crawling or crouching
On the dining table
Thirty percent is allocated.
On the dining table, thirty percent is allocated.

Let not the hatchery and breast milk determine my performance,
Let not the fibre and beads I weave determine my scores,   Let
not the yams I pound determine my CV,
The cultural map says lullaby is the sole chapter on my page,
Yet with spears and dogs, I hunted and caught harmattan locusts.

Mushrooming Mushrooms

Life grows and blooms outside lines of prints,
And flowers and blossoms in the suburbs of the mind.
Life flocks and flourishes in trackless forests;
Life incubates and germinates in the jungles of the mind,
Life swarms and streams beyond the restrictions of sight,
And take roots and propagates behind constructed boundaries.

Life swims and sails outside erected mountains,
And leaps over huddles and threatening barricades;
Life lives and metamorphose outside bolted borders;
And roves and roams outside cultural CVs,
Life struggles to survive during the storms of tradition,
And remains its own pillar in the swerve of hurricanes.

So why still remain a slave to sight?
When the psyche language and customs had veiled
With thick shrouds of shadows and masks,
Has been unmasked and facades lifted off.

So why still a slave to the language of breasts and beards.
Ferret out the less-tapped entrails of the colony within,
In trails are brain children of her fecundity clock;
For the sterility dramatized
Her Curriculum Vitae has dismissed.

June 2012

March 8

Like soldiers they troop
Out of the shadows to light,
A journey whose strides
Reside in appointments,
A journey whose strides
Erected in achievements.

Like termites they throng
Out of the smoke to sun rays,
A journey whose strides
Immortalized in access,
A journey whose strides
Memorialized in ladders.

Like grasshoppers they comb,
Every bush path they search,
A journey whose strides
Commemorated in March 8th,
A journey whose strides
Engendered in awareness.

Like hunters they foraged
Every farmland for mental suckle,
For the battle must be won
With words they must war,
For the battle must be won
With pregnant ballot boxes.

War with Words

War with words
War with voice
War with ink
For with the war of words
Far and wide echoes roar.

War with words
War with voice
War with ink
For when the seeds of liberty with clothes of dialogue are sewn,
Mentality is restructured within the ambit of marriage in diversity.

War with words
War with voice
War with ink
Bury words and verses of mass destruction,
For when the era of cultural categorizing is frozen in the heart, And
from arm solution to dialogue embraced;
From smoke chamber to the powerhouse reside,
From charcoal cottage to electrified flats lodged,
From bungalows to citadels boarded,
From bamboo huts to bastions roomed,
From tenants to landlords become,
Then from boundaries to bunching become.

The Journey

From now on women from weavers to builders become,
From now on the margins from menders to makers become,
From now on the colony within, from silence to architects become,
From now on the masses from messengers to managers become,
From now on the half-baked from consumers to inventors become,
From now on learners from harvesters to authors become,
From now on commentators from critics to writers become,
From now on women from cleaners to constructors become,
From now on women from child-bearers to creators become,
And henceforth the hands from labour to manufacturers become.

From now on;
She carves her own CV further than the raging indigenous vocabulary
allows,
She writes her own history beyond the boundaries set by the furious
ethnic linguistics,
She builds her own home outside the restrains imposed by the cultural
Birth Certificates;
And plays the drum conceived and carved with our matted- wedded
thoughts,
For the mound is moulded with multi-layered entangled hands.

❀ ❀

No Longer on Stage

No longer on stage,
Compelled by grey-bearded customs
To perform programmed roles,
No longer on stage,
Programmed like stage actors
Never to sing out of tone.

No longer on stage
Coerced by unhealthy customs
To dance to the rhythm of Kwifo and Mwerong,
No longer in the shadows
Waiting to execute the rumblings of tradition.

No longer on stage
Squatting at the foot of the trunk
And nodding to decisions and conclusions,
No longer in the dark
Cowering like crickets
While vultures hover above their heads.

No longer on stage,
Shrinking with fright at the sight of red-feather mountains,
Trembling and nodding to choices and verdicts,
Like sprouting tongues of green palm fronds caressed by breeze,
Hunkering forward to yield to the direction of the storm,
For its knocks and blows were taboo subjects for public ears.

No longer on stage
Trembling like leaves in the hands of roaring tempests,
No longer on stage
Shrinking like rivers in the heart of dry seasons.

No longer on stage
Programmed to nurse the nurseries
While Anthills roar and roam,
No longer on stage
Programmed to pound with pestles
And trained to grind pepper with stones.

No longer in the dark
Squatting like mushrooms at the foot of mountains
No longer in the dark
Crawling like beggars to pick falling crumbs,
From the top of the master's dining table.

Welcome to the dining table;
Thinking together and sowing together,
For the future must we together plant,
Welcome to the dining table,
For access and awareness must we
In the same measure embrace.

Poems on Social Ills, Ethics and Religious Morality

❋ ❋

Judgement Day

When at the threshold of Judgement Day,
Like a slaughter house your report card will be bleeding,
And from the womb of your report card
A continuous streaming of premenstrual menstruation,
Because extra-large pregnant pockets with financial obesity afflicted,
Because your financial hive from financial constipation blighted,
Because your financial garner stashed in foreign soils excavated.
While awaiting deportation order and appropriate action;
Your growth clock from cardiac arrest will convulse,
While your heart like tremors will tremble,
Invading your ears like roaring earthquakes,
And annexing your ears like the sound of pounding hooves.

When at the threshold of Judgement Day,
The bells of emergence begin to ring,
The hammer of the Law will unleash its venom
Because like the side belly of an expectant goat;
Stick out looted heavy-weight pockets in regal command;
Both young and old, the rich and the poor,
Partisans and coaches, facilitators and middlemen,
Even referees and match fixers,
Your pages will be burrowed and hollowed out and exhumed
And like source you will be scooped out and ferried away.

When at the threshold of Judgement Day,
The gates of Kondengui flung open its fangs;
Ready to swallow small and big fishes;
Ready to consume midges and elephants,
Ready to strangle architects and swindlers,
Ready to expose arbitrators and adjudicators,
Ready to unearth hawkers of marks and endangered species,

For morals are in danger of erosion,
And values in danger of corrosion;
Legal daggers will rage above heads,
To stem the tides of moral extinction.

When at the threshold of Judgement Day,
Your CV bleeds like a slaughter house,
Your pages like infected leaves will wither in size,
Still your work ethics like pus from ulcers will smell and smell.
And when your tears like floods will flow unend,
 And your body gripped by fountains of feverish fears;
Because the claws of the Law must assault your bones,
And leave in its trail a frenzy of emotions,
Tearing through your flesh like the pains of parturition;
Because public pulse became private wallet
And was impounded and taken hostage;
Because corrosive breed must be nipped on the bud;
Legal Creeds will summon all to Judgment.
Above your heads will swing legal swords
Ready to stab and release a sting,
For venom will be spewed where corruption germinated.

When the Lord of Judgment will sit on high throne,
And at his Court of First Instance we gather like refugees;
And shock waves in our spines penetrating like bad news;
Without fear or favour, and without consideration for name and skin
pigment,
Hawkers and road-side vendors will render an account;
Teachers and preachers will render an account;
Tax collectors and Bankers will render an account:
The ladder of command and the Red-feather Chiefs,
The tree and its roots and the Black and Red Feathers.
For Judgment will be pronounced on the trunk and the roots,
For Judgment will be pronounced on the mighty and the mean,
For Judgment will be pronounced on elephants and midges.

Like red coal some hearts will glow and groan,
Still some hearts will pound and gallop and dance,
And like clothes of trees shivering in the wind
The world in your mirror will whirl in fits of feverish epilepsy.
For fear of being flushed out of mountainous habitats;
For fear of being weeded out of state plantations;
Or even for fear of being wrenched out of financial estates;
For 1PM and 5 PM News Headlines often stage earthquakes of the heart.
Because pregnant pockets suffer from financial constipation;
Because report cards bleed like a delivery ward,
Because auto-evaluation CVs look like a butcher's slab.

When at the threshold of Judgement Day,
The Almighty Legal Creeds will mount the throne of Judgment,
Like flags your accomplishments will be hoisted,
Like anthills your achievements will be erected,
Like parasites your failings will be rejected,
Like infections your concoctions will be accomplices,
Like pollution your files will be impurities,
Like sin your oaths will be blasphemies.

When at the threshold of Judgement Day,
The Almighty Legal Sword will mount the throne of Judgment,
Like bedbugs your signatures will be accomplices,
Like Ebola your relics will be corpses,
Like extremist groups, your achievements will be vanity,
Like excrement, tappers will be flushed out,
And like the full length of a river,
Your lies and libels will be trails of evidence.

When at the threshold of the Verdict Day,
Afraid to hear *relever de ses fonctions*:
Relieve of your duties, or reduction in grade,
For fear of being flushed out of blossoming hives,

Since appointments plant ulcers in the hearts of many;
In your pants your manhood will sweat and shudder,
Like the nipples of blooms in caressing hands of breeze.
Like volcanic convulsions your heartbeat will tremble,
Like swelling tremors your body will quiver and convulse,
Like a withered body whose blood tracks have collapsed
Urine will glide down your legs and slide along your feet;
Like mud slide a pool of diarrhoea-stricken stools will dart down your
legs;
And in fright your stomach will rumble and wobble.
With feverish gesticulations your fingers and garments,
Will shiver like clothes of trees in the breeze,
Because your godfathers would have vanished
Like healing herbs at the sight of a corpse,
Because your godfathers would have vanished
Like a thief at the sound of gunshots,
Because your godfathers would have vanished
Like an adulterer from the laps of a colonized colony.

When at the threshold of Judgement Day,
The Legal Dagger will mount the throne of Judgment,
And in a thunderous tone declares a death penalty;
Like a mountain humbled by an eruption,
Your pride will begin to blink and shrink,
Like epileptic heartbeats of quaking mountains.
And still like a blank and naked map,
Your page will look like bare and barren soils.
And like a debtor hiding from creditors,
The door of your stomach will be shot even at lunchtime.
When at the threshold of Judgement Day,
While some wait for appointments,
Some will not avoid disappointments;
While some wait for promotion,
Some will not avoid relegation;
And while some wait for installation allowances

Some will be promised death allowances.
But where labourers tilt and toiled,
And the harvest is ready for garnering,
Body language and frenzied gesticulations,
Will announce those shortlisted,
For the next lap of the race.

September 2015

The Most Sumptuous Dangerous Meal I

Gripped by the cramps of that barbaric thirst,
Was the night they were betrayed,
And the very night they were decayed,
Was the very night the flesh was in tears.
Like medicine that aggravates the disease it heals,
From their veiled abodes they took out the muddled meal,
And like ravenous dogs during seasons of carnal traffic,
Gave it to their baits and said:
Eat it and share it to (wo) men,
So that wherever you serve
The sumptuous dangerous meal,
Shall like a muddy tributary will be muddled.
Remember this, as a pre-emptive caution to hunger of the loins.

In the eyes of physicians,
Through the lens of theologians,
Or the mirror of parents,
It is forbidden to have canal knowledge of an unripe human.
So many infected ingredients went into the making
Of the most sumptuous dangerous meal,
And the most sumptuous meal
Was the most dangerous meal;
And the most sumptuous meal
Was the muddiest meal.

The Most Sumptuous Dangerous Meal II

On another cock's dominion he feasted his eyes,
In another colony's pillar she gripped with greed,
But the bums and thighs or the whispers and sighs,
Or the glares and tempests of such sour joys,
Were treasured theatres for sour comedies,
And also treasured theatres for tragic comedies.
Just like scratching and hugging were the sacrilegious methodology
For harvesting faulty and infected data.

Still ungodly and illegal, still unethical and immoral
The shameless methodology for collecting contaminated juice
Which parents and moral crusaders call toxic nectar
Was winking and smiling and flattery and adulation.
And the most sumptuous meal
Was the most dangerous meal;
And the most sumptuous meal
Was the most muddled meal.

On another cock's dominion he feasted his eyes,
In another colony's pillar she gripped with greed,
Unknown to the cock and hen, was a raging storm in stock,
Which like burbles of boiling anger threatening to explode in the chest,
Or like a twirl of magma in the pregnant womb of Lake Nyos;
And like a whirl of Ebola in the quagmire of River Ebola,
Was preparing the stage for tragic eruption.
Unknown to the horse and rider, was the surging tempest;
Which like cantankerous lava in the bosom of Mount Fako;
Or like glowing discharges under the terrorist leadership of volcanic energy;
Was setting the stage for an endemic explosion.
And the most sumptuous meal

Was the most dangerous meal;
And the most sumptuous meal
Was the most muddled meal.

Unknown to the adventurers was the inflaming defecations,
Unknown to the thieves was a gurgle of raging feelings,
Which like a flurry of agitating bubbles on the surface of boiling water;
Or like a surge in the arrival of migrants,
And like swelling debris from furious bush fires,
Or even like pecking heat from angry sun rays,
Was preparing the body for an endemic invasion.

Unknown to the Adam and Eve was the lurking magma,
Which like harmful insects threatening to invade Empire boundaries;
Or like religious earthquake hovering over Africa's peaceful skies;
Or even like toxic smoke from industries and bush fires,
And still like suicide bombers who masked like masqueraders;
Was setting the stage for an epidemic detonation.
And the most sumptuous meal
Was the most dangerous meal;
And the most sumptuous meal
Was the most muddled meal.

Unknown to the explorers was the infected meal;
Which like hums and buzzes of bombs on suicidal operations;
Or like gruesome-face measles in the palms of afflicted leaves;
Or like a suspect awaiting results of that dreaded virus;
Or like a Suspect awaiting the Court's verdict on Judgment Day,
Or even like the heart-rending 5 PM Appointments News Headlines;
Often accompanied by heavy downpours of laughter and tears
Was setting the stage for a roaring eviction.
And the most sumptuous meal
Was the most dangerous meal;
And the most sumptuous meal
Was the most muddled meal.

Unknown to the blind tourists was a battalion of effusive stings;
Which like roasting pains of parturition in the habitat of the hive of
children,
Or like frenzied pains welling up and darting across intestinal tracks,
Was setting the theatre for precipitated miscarriage.
And the most sumptuous meal
Was the most dangerous meal;
And the most sumptuous meal
Was the most muddled meal.

During the unholy performance,
Into hen was unleashed and buried;
What garbage heaps fear to lodge;
Or what surgeons scan using hand boots.
Because like the forbidden fruit;
So was the prohibited food;
Forbidden to unripe fans.
And the most sumptuous meal
Was the most dangerous meal;
And the most sumptuous meal
Was the most muddled meal.

On that night super was served,
Just like the night they were betrayed;
The meal they were served,
Which they devoured with famish greed;
Was polluted and infected like toxic consciousness.
And the most sumptuous meal
Was the most dangerous meal;
And the most sumptuous meal
Was the most muddled meal.

Like a warrior he invaded,
Like a storm he stormed
Into many beds they leaped;

Into another grave he plunged.
Unknown to the boundaries of sight,
Was the lurking volcano,
For into that toilet was buried;
A multitude of magma,
And a swarm of stings from soldier ants;
Brought from other explorations,
Which for fools are expeditions;
For the ponds where he swarm,
Were swarming with worms and weevils;
And wobbling with millions of millipedes;
And like a battalion of bees;
Stung and tingled with lavish immunity.
And the most sumptuous meal
Was the most dangerous meal;
And the most sumptuous meal
Was the most muddled meal.

On the night super was served;
In dozes they savoured the sea of diseases,
Like gluttons they demolished
Mountainous platefuls of maggots;
But as the juicy meal infected was,
So their budding bosoms affected were.
Firmly planted in the inner region to germinate and colonize;
Firmly planted in channels of production and propagation
To bloom and proliferate and propagate toxic waste;
Firmly incubated in blood branches to hatch and hide pollution;
Were vipers and raiders and predators and burglars.
For the most sumptuous meal
Was the most dangerous meal;
And the most sumptuous meal
Was the most muddled meal.

Like red spots on sick pale leaves,
Like germs creeping up the veins of infected leaves;
So were their skins encrusted.
Just like their blood tributaries were corrupted,
So did their tattoo skins with rashes erupted.
And the most sumptuous meal
Was the most dangerous meal;
And the most sumptuous meal
Was the most muddled meal.

With scabies and rabies their skins were besmeared;
With millipedes and centipedes their barks were besmirched,
Like sneezing laps their foreheads with furrows were furrowed;
As if besieged by stinging bees their skins had developed decaying
growths.
Like the buttocks of a new born
Suffering from protracted contact with wetness and faeces
Their red-brick coloured faces were laminated with scars and scabs;
Like jagged eruptions on the skin of a porcupine
Stubs had smeared their arms and fingers.
In lengthened wraithlike shapes,
Lay shocking images even very eerie to look at.
A chill wind of fright crept up my blood routes.
My spine was chilled and my hairs raised.
I knew for sure that the empire of diseases
They harvested from other toilets,
Were the children of the unholy alliance.
And the most sumptuous meal
Was the most dangerous meal;
And the most sumptuous meal
Was the most muddled meal.

On their necks and arms and hands and bare skins,
What looked like caterpillar sized craggy toothed scars
Had tunnelled through the flesh leaving dark hunched warts;

What looked like snaking dark worms into their flesh had burrowed,
Leaving thick meandering lumps that looked like serrated tree grafts;
What looked like black jagged beetles curling on stubs of rugged tree
trunks,
Or like swollen noodles hanging down on the angry necks of hoary
trees,
Had coated their bodies leaving as trails
Baffled ribs and bulges of tissues bulging around the necklines.
Were human necks bearing small calabashes?
Was it the human voice that spoke to spectators
Or the hiss of insects and disease-stricken fowls?
Had human bodies transformed into dead trunks of palm trees?
A sea of thoughts and answered questions wavered across my mind
As I watched with fright the cadaverous forms hissing like dry winds.
And the most sumptuous meal
Was the most dangerous meal;
And the most sumptuous meal
Was the most muddled meal.

Colonized by god fire,
Which spews verminous gunfire;
Their faces with ridges looked landscaped,
For the salacious meal they relished,
And the meal they cherished,
Was swarming with pests and predators,
And with vermin and scavengers.
For the most dangerous meal,
Like the Lord's Supper,
Was their last supper.
And the most sumptuous meal
Was the most dangerous meal;
And the most sumptuous meal
Was the most muddled meal.

Three months after the meal, three months after the performance,
Like potholes turned to gullies; like gaping holes on walls after a war;
So was the bleeding anus like a canal flow.
With catarrh-like stools, was the ground around trailed;
With invading breath, which cause people to switch their nostrils from side to side,
So was the air above our heads polluted;
Like napkins on the eroded buttocks of diarrhoea-stricken babies,
Were the tattered diapers on their fading buttocks sullied.
Like squashed fruits on bony trunks of trees,
So was their flesh thirsty and pale.
And like trails of catarrh, was the bedside littered.
Like withered trees whose leaves at dry season shed,
Were their shrunken bodies bare and barren, or lean and declined;
Because the home which should act as Day Care Centre,
Refused to babysit the cadaverous forms,
And became for dupes and preys a nest of thorns.
Hard to survive the shock of shame, the cadaverous forms
And on their death beds an oath of sealed lips taken;
And the most sumptuous meal
Was the most dangerous meal;
And the most sumptuous meal
Was the most muddled meal.

Three months after the meal, three months after the performance,
Though still hatchlings their hopes were butchered and dreams ulcerated,
Soon their clock began to tick;
Soon their intestines twirled and belched,
For ailing species must be extinguished.
Like frenzied fire whose flames rises furiously into the sky,
Or gruesome clouds hovering above like vultures,
Their feverish fears, with anger began to whirl with fumes.
In the deserted chamber they were imprisoned;
And like ferocious rain pouring from the sky;

The anus was sighing and yawning and vomiting and leaking;
For dogs and flies it was delight to trail the trails.
For friends and foes trooping in and out,
Or groups and tourists who flood their room;
To gape with fright at the tattooed occupants;
Their darkly lit cavity became an attraction;
For the stories they harvested;
And the juicy subject matter was that:
"No seed nor family nor name survived."
And the most sumptuous meal
Was the most dangerous meal;
And the most sumptuous meal
Was the most muddled meal.
Soon the shrieks of women were head across villages,
Because the storm had wrenched off the roofs above heads.
When the hen and cock were nipped in the bud,
And laid in state like lifeless woods;
At the threshold of Heaven,
The damned souls were summoned.
While to the Bible the meal was a sin;
And to Judges the meal was unlawful,
According to Tradition and Custom,
The marriage was concocted without libation.
While to parents the victims were poisoned;
And to the soothsayer the couple was bewitched;
To sympathizers, it was TB,
Whereas to the tourist, it was the serpent.

While to lovers of drama the plot was weaved on the forbidden fruit;
And to the hand that caved the tale and its branches
The actions of the hero and heroine provided a plot for tragedy;
To surgeons they were nipped on the bud by SIDA.

While to Satan they ate to multiply,
And to me their death was a lesson,

To Natural Law the law of nature must be respected,
Although some school of thought holds that
Guilt in one system of Law,
Is innocence in another code of Law.
To all green and unripe fans,
Open your eyes, but close your minds;
For the most sumptuous meal,
Is the most muddled meal.

🏵 🏵

At The Tribunal of Ethics and Conscience

Dramatis Personae

God:	Supreme Judge
Man of God:	Plaintiff
Barrister Society:	Lawyer to the Plaintiff

Darwin, Sigmund Freud,
Karl Marx, Jean-Paul Satre,
Machiavelli (Barrister Mach),
Nietzsche, Feuerbach: The Accused and Self-Imposed Lawyers

The two Youths: Boy and girl.

Barrister Society: Mr. Sigmund Freud; look at these two fading youths standing before this Honourable Panel of Jurists.

Their bodies are colonized by ribs and veins;
The walls of their necks look like the craggy barks of a kolanut tree at an advanced state of menopause;

The waning flesh on their bodies is weevilled and burrowed through by scars with the shape of millipedes;

Their skins look like the red-patchy buttocks of top soil that has suffered prolongation of soil erosion;
Their necks and skins are smeared with red-brick-colour scars;

The colour of their bony skins look like the buttocks of a new-born baby suffering from protracted contact with faeces and wetness;…

Barrister Mach: *(Interrupts).* And how is my learned client responsible for such a shocking portrayal of human wreckage?

Barrister Society: The ID and EGO are Sigmund Freud's brain children;

The two propagandas are responsible for the upsurge in aggressive energies and unwanted pregnancies in this religious community;

They are also responsible for the propagation of Sexually Transmissible Marks and Diseases in this God-fearing land!

My Lord, the Academy of Psychoanalysis is undeniably a threat to the campaign on **"AIDS FREE SOCIETY AND SECURITY FOR ALL"!**…

Barrister Mach: *(Interrupts).* Objection, My Lord!

God: Objection overruled. Barrister Society may continue.

Barrister Society: Thank you My Lord. Nietzsche, you rejected Christian dogma and called it an arsenal of lies and nihilism;

Jean Paul Sartre, your unmistakable atheistic and essentialist articulations are not only assaults on ethics and religion;

They are assaults on these two misguided youths.

And you-Karl Marx and Feuerbach;

Your disregard for religion has fuelled disbelief in the existence of God and divine mediation in human affairs.

Darwin, your theory of evolution is a challenge to the Biblical notion of creation.

My learned colleagues, your philosophies are alluring addictions;

They are responsible for the trails of displaced school dropouts;

And accompanying consequences of exposure to enrolment into gangs,

And cults and invasive groups!

They are responsible for the unfolding scene of savagery;

Creeping and crawling into communities;

Around you and me are human shadows scampering for safety.

My learned colleagues, you will not deny that your toxic doctrines are the very foundations of disbelief in God and life after death;

You cannot deny that your school is a factory where toxic ideologies are planted and nurtured!

Of course, you cannot also deny that your endemic pedagogy is the root cause of eruptions and ethical abscesses that have left ethically gaping potholes on the walls of society!...

Barrister Mach: Objection my Lord!

God: Objection dismissed.

Barrister Mach: Barrister Society, do you have any prove for such damaging allegations against our worldwide acclaimed and most privileged core curricula courses?

Barrister Society: Of course yes. My Lord, atheistic, essentialist and ID driven pedagogies are famous for hatching pestilential, poisonous and endemic ideologies!

Such a pedagogy issues license permits and authorizations that cause untamed instincts to indulge in barbaric acts of transgressions and sexual adventures irrespective of age, health factor and marital status!

God:	Charges convincing and arguments sustainable and defensible!
Barrister Mach:	Barrister Society, your charges dishonour worldwide acclaimed curative and remedial pedagogies! My Lord, that my clients issue permits, I do not dispute the fact. But the point must be made that a Permit or License is an authorization and not an obligation!
Barrister Society:	Barrister Mach, according to the Holy Book of Law, whoever, through philosophy or propaganda, acting as accomplice or a motivation, hatches or supports doctrines that are likely to promote depravity, cause moral injury; And endanger health, is predisposed to prosecution! According to the same Book of Law still, whoever and in whatever way, Encourages the planting, nursing, germination and propagation of toxic propagandas shall be punished with a death penalty!
Barrister Mach:	My learned colleague! My clients are accused of issuing philosophically-oriented propagandist licenses;

That is true! My Lord, it may be important to caution that issuing a License or Permit does not make one a criminal!

The Book of Law says an accused is assumed innocent until proven guilty by the Court of Law.

My learned colleague! Don't be surprise if such disparaging and unfounded allegations earn for you and your Plaintiff an accommodation in jail!

Barrister Society: My learned colleague! Be informed that when a License or Permit;

Is a motivation behind a crime, it becomes an accomplice in that very crime!

Barrister Mach: Objection my Lord, I wish to reiterate the point that my clients issue authorizations and not obligations!

God: Objection overruled!

Barrister Society: Thank you My Lord. My learned colleague and clients,

Be informed that every Permit should have a Restriction!

The ID, EGO and essentialist and atheistic propagandas are toxic fertilizers; They are endemic maternities that manufacture and ensure the breeding,

And propagation of seductive anti social stimulants!

Visible consequences are barbarism and Sexually Tapped and Sexually Transmitted Diseases!

My Lord, the flourishing of barbarism and diseases, despite attempts to program their burial, is sufficient testimony that instincts are encouraged by toxic dogmas to indulge in barbaric acts of violence and sexual misadventures!

My dear misleading pedagogues! Would you really deny that your school and its subjects guarantee the breeding and transmission of body and social invaders?

Man of God: Another Shakespearean Daniel has come to judgement!

Praise the Lord! Alleluia!

God: I will not tolerate any form of rowdiness in my Honourable Court!

Barrister Mach: Thank You my Lord.

My Lord, my high profiled client sitting before this Honourable Panel in the name of Sigmund Freud gave birth to the Super Ego.

His highly acclaimed course 'The Super Ego' is a restriction to what this half-baked critic calls 'toxic dogmas and barbaric acts of violence and sexual misadventures'!

Barrister Society: The Book of Law says whoever trains, motivates or pressurizes body emotions, and through propaganda,

To cause or participate in acts of depravity is guilty and deserves to be punished!

The same Book of Law says ignorance before the law is not an excuse!

Barrister Mach: My Lord, a discipline with pedagogic and healing potentials like the Super Ego should be considered a warning that love out of marriage is prohibited!...

Barrister Society: Objection My Lord! By Ethical and Moral Standards,

A warning, I repeat, is a restriction and not a prohibition!

Consequently, those anti-social nests and trappings that posture under alluring appellations such as Atheism, Evolution, Survival of the Fittest,

And the ID and Ego do not, in any way, and by any means,

Signal the life span, beginning of obligation; end of restrictions;

And expiring dates for its Opiums and Permits!

My learned colleague assumes that the so-called 'pedagogy-oriented Super Ego' is a warning that love before marriage is prohibited!

He needs to know that a prohibition alone does not in any way signal any threats of danger and expiry date! I rest my Case, My Lord...

Barrister Mach: Barrister Society, this is gross misinterpretation of acclaimed research findings!

Besides, my clients issue authorizations and not obligations!

My Lord, You need to withdraw the Certificate of Critical Worthiness you issued to Barrister Society until he is able to make a distinction between an authorization and an obligation!...

Barrister Society: Objection My Lord!

God: Sustained!

Man of God:	Amen!
Barrister Society:	My Good Lord; can anyone deny that Evolution, Atheism, propaganda, and the ID and EGO pedagogies are the very herbs that create the cancer they seek to heal?;
	My Lord! Can any right thinking individual deny that those pedagogic propagandas and trappings are the very manure that feed cocoa and coffee leaves with the infected pests they are expected to eradicate?
God:	You sound more convincing, Barrister Society.
Barrister Mach:	I raise an objection here! Mr. Lord! Remember Your Holy Bible says:
	"Go ye to the world and multiply".
Darwin:	Barrister Mach is undeniably one of the rare species of Academic Legal Critics with unrivalled intellectual virility;
	The Almighty God should answer his question!
God:	Does the phrase 'multiply' means 'sex before marriage'?
Barrister Mach:	My Lord, the target audience should be blamed for abusing Research Findings!

Barrister Society: My Lord, it is now clear to this Tribunal of Conscience that delinquency, Sex before marriage and other forms of moral infections are motivated by "Philosophical Permits and Licenses" issued by the controversial and anti-religious ideologies hatched by academically fertile philosophies!

The ID, Ego, Atheism and other toxic opiums should be wrenched off from School curriculums lest they continue to wreck untold havoc in human society!

Darwin, Sigmund Freud, Karl Marx, Jean-Paul Satre, Machiavelli, Nietzsche, Feuerbach: We raise an objection here. Our good Lord, according to the Law of Theory and Criticism, whoever lives and dies without giving birth to theories and propagandas is academically bare and barren;

And will not have their name cradled in the Canon of Great Thinkers.

God: It is now very clear to this unrivalled Tribunal of Ethics and Conscience that the addictive and moral butchers that gushed out of the mental laps of these philosophers are intoxications!

Man of God: Amen!

God: Barrister Society may continue with cross-examination.

Barrister Society: Thank you My Lord.

Dear philosophers of unquestionable intellectual acumen;

You developed toxic and blasphemous dogmas,

You disguised them and worked hard to ensure their propagation;

Your intention was to get your target audience to be part of a group that has been established to commit acts that are contrary to religious teachings!...

Barrister Mach: Objection My Lord!

The right of my clients to dignity and freedom of academic religion is violated by libels and damaging descriptions!

God: Barrister Society may continue.

Barrister Society: Thank You My Lord;

Machiavelli, your alluring doctrines have no other objective than incite rebellion against the Holy Book of Law;

Mr. Nietzsche, the visible consequences of your shocking claim that 'God is dead' are: terrorism and extremism in ramifications such as: bombing, hostage taking, kidnapping, banditry, greed, jealousy, hatred, killing, bribery, and corruption;

Mr. Sigmund Freud, these two youths are infected by your doctrines!

Dear high profiled philosophers;

All of you have sinned against God in one way or another and in different degrees of emphasis…

Barrister Mach: Objection My Lord! This is not a religious issue! We cannot use Religious Law in a purely Academic Trial!

God: This is my verdict. As the cure for the damage the identified contagious pedagogies have caused human society,

The biological parents and practitioners of propagandas will either have to revise the concerned courses and trim off the excesses,

Or have their subjects brutally wrenched off from school and religious curriculums!

Barrister Mach: My Lord, is this the reward my clients deserve for discovering the cure for illiteracy and ignorance?

God: When the cure for a disease has more side effects than healing effects;

There is need for either pruning or a ban!;

I hold strongly to my position that the alleged cure for illiteracy and ignorance is a challenge to religious morality!

Barrister Mach: This is religious intolerance!;

My Lord; the right of my clients to freedom of academic religion is unlawfully carted away!

God: When a palm tree starts producing fermented palm wine;

There is need to crop off the old bamboo branches if fecundity or rejuvenation is what consumers desire!

In other words, propagandas that challenge religious teaching must be nipped on the bud!

Barrister Mach: We have to be careful as to whether an action constitutes a religious bridge, a bridge of ethics, or a bridge of academic codified standards!

God: My audience, all contagious propagandas and pedagogies including atheism and survival of the fittest are threats to consumer safety!;

The addictive and moral butchers we erroneously perceive as the cure for illiteracy and ignorance are intoxications and need thorough detoxification! My word is the Law!

Barrister Mach: Where is the place of freedom of religious worship in this trial?

God: Barrister Mach! You are guilty of contempt of Court! Court!

(Curtain closes with Sigmund Freud, Darwin, Machiavelli, Karl Marx, Feuerbach, Jean Paul Sartre and Nietzsche trooping towards the Court of Appeal.)

Vaccinate the Judiciary

Vaccinate the Law Lords,
Heal influence peddling proceedings,
Dignifying it is to survive the surgery,
While still in the theatre.
For when like an aborted malformed foetus Justice is retailed,
Justice is tethered while truth is roped.

Vaccinate the Judiciary
Sterilize Lawyers and Adjudicators,
Dignifying it is to mend where into shreds you severed,
For when the thief is protected and the owner indicted,
Justice is detained while guilt is retained.

Vaccinate the Judiciary
Unveil the veiled and concocted evidence,
Dignifying it is to cause the convict to sterilize where they muddled,
Than trade Justice to the highest bidder.
For when the culprit in the Courtroom sings songs of triumph
And the innocent in the Courtroom sheds tears of sorrow
Justice is hawked and truth is detained.

Vaccinate the Judiciary,
Immunize the viper and the hatchings when the viper has hatched,
Dignifying it is to heal endemic corruption than water its seeds,
For when the robber snores and the robbed groans and laments
Justice is marketed and truth is caged.

Vaccinate Civil Society Activists and heal their prejudice,
Dignifying it is to use the same critical lens on top dogs and low dogs,

For when for the sake of fame, the terrorist is vindicated
While the terrorized is attacked,
Justice is denied while prejudice is adored.

❀ ❀

Vaccinate the Continent

Vaccinate the continent
Heal abscesses and ailments on the walls of its body,
Vaccinate the continent
Heal the flare-ups and eruptions in the heart of its nations.

Vaccinate Tradition,
Heal its excesses,
Vaccinate tradition
Heal unhealthy customs.

Vaccinate Bankers and Tax Collectors,
Heal their robbing tactics,
Vaccinate Tax Inspectors,
Heal their tapping strategies.

Vaccinate the Media, Print Media and the Social Media
Sterilize speculative conclusions and postings,
Sanitize defamations and smears and blasphemies,
And filter their words when they raise an alarm.
Their noble duty be not to intoxicate the public through malignant
propaganda.
Although gate keepers and monitoring machines they are,
They should raise alarm without insulting
Else the victimized could shout louder or raise a sting.

Purify religious comedians and disinfect miracles,
And heal their performances.
Disinfect the afflicted and heal their curses.
Cleanse anointed comedians and castrate their drama.
For when miracles are dramatized, propagandist they become.

Vaccinate the teachers,
Heal half-baked cakes.
Vaccinate researchers,
Sanitize the garbage
Emasculate Plagiarism,
And garbage out the garbaged in.

Vaccinate diviners, and sanitize their concoctions
Sanitize their miracles and decontaminate the contaminated.
Vaccinate soaring ambition and heal its extravagances,
Vaccinate effusive feelings, and heal their outburst.
Vaccinate turbulent emotions and heal its contagious excesses,
Vaccinate hurdling instincts and tame their gluttony.
Vaccinate kidnappers and strangle their strategies.

Sterilize the brain child of the imagination,
Spruce off linguistic abscesses,
Decontaminate the academic maternity,
And bowdlerize propaganda and hate-preaching.

The Stage

Sculptors and carvers
On stage are actors,
And programmed roles performed;
For when the sculptor carves
And the mask must be on
And his cast is done
Life becomes a stage
And everyone a role assigned.

Like midst art thou
Like vapour art thou
Like haze art thou
Like miasma art thou
Like an actor art thou
Because we all
Are actors and travellers.

Bleeding the Heart of Africa Dry

The race for "Gombo" is in its full gear.
In the silent hours of the dark tappers lurk around
Along the corridors of juicy habitats they crawl in suits;
Milking nations and draining Anthems,
Extracting the nutrients which feed the Nation's blood streams,
Draining the energy which feeds the pores on the skins of Anthems.
Payrolls infested with Ghost-workers,
Payrolls flooding with Bush Fallers,
Payrolls inundated with corpses,
Because the race for "Gombo" is in its full gear.

Because the race for "Gombo" is in its full gear,
The once overflowing river now shrivelling and shrinking
And the ribs and bones on the chests of nations are exposed;
The once brimming breasts on the chests of Anthems
Are dehydrating and withering,
The once spilling over fountain now leaking
And the lungs of nations are dry and thirsty.
The once fecund womb of Africa now barren
The lungs of states are perforated;
The blood streams of nations fast dehydrating and desiccating.
The pillars on which we lean withering, shrivelling, and shrinking
The legs on which we walk are limping and staggering
The sap that feeds our stomachs bleeding dry,
For the juice on which we suckle is draining.
Like brimful-streams and lakes withering because of climate change,
The baobab may one day shrink in breath and body build
And when the pores on Africa's skin are blinking,
For multiple salary codes were shouldered by one person,
Complicity, collusion and venality,
The holes through which State coffers are sapped,

And now poverty announces itself,
Despite efforts from Government to strangle corruption.

The race for "Gombo" is in its full gear
Yet constipation awaits corrosive pockets.
For when census is conducted, as it is often done,
In the wagon of morally infected and wrecked souls
Illegal extraction, draining, tapping, and milking
Will all be garbaged in and caged.
Your time is up! Roars the legal dagger,
For the state payroll must be sieved!
Your coffin is sealed! Decrees the legal dagger,
For practitioners must be flushed out,
And the corrupt must soon read its own obituary.

The Diseased Stricken Road

Chorus
The very first rains after your birth,
In butchered fabric thou are clad;
One season after your birth,
In fragmented array thou art decked;
Only one rain has fallen over your head,
Only one sun over your thinly festooned flesh,
You look already sick and needs a healer.
Be patient my patient,
For your surgeon only comes when your gaping grave is dug.

Like a tortoise's shell, or the bark of a trunk;
With just one slap or just one kick;
Your hard bark is battered and panel beaten.
With one timid thud from well-nourished tyres;
With simple blows and knocks from pregnant tankers,
Or modest bumps and punches from obese trucks,
With retiring kicks and thumps from hoofs and boots,
Your cake-iced skin looks butchered.

With measles and scabies your skin is colonized,
At your tender age, faster you faded;
Like a bleached face, rapidly you eroded,
Before your first birthday, sooner you declined.
Twenty days after your birth, numbered are your days.

And as the signs of life are gaping graves,
And the signs of tracks are yawning lakes,
Spectators and Reporters call you pit toilets,
While users and passers-by call you death traps;
Because before your first birthday,

Your rooms are housed with mud and staring pools.

Your coated flesh has become crusted,
Your cracked skin has become sunken,
And your features fissured and fractured.
Your clefts and cracks are soon ruptured,
Your gutters with filth are well lodged.

In the warm embrace of stagnant mud;
In the warm cuddle of staring pools,
In the warm grip of silent swamps,
Sank cues of Lorries in muddy lakes.
Like the Mediterranean that has become a cemetery for migrants,
Bystanders call you a cemetery for tyres.

Because your crumpled face is encrusted;
Architects say your body was thinly decked,
Because your thin lanes are brutally butchered,
The contractor claim his budget was slaughtered,
For many fingers were soiled in the budget butchery.

Your lanes with abscesses propagating,
Your skin with diseases populating,
Your tar with scabies infected,
Your lanes with gutters gaping,
Your channels with pools inundated,
And sores and wounds, or blisters and eruptions,
Are all your disorders and signs of malady.

Your tars like rags into shreds are rendered,
Your tracks with garbage unruffled and hoarded,
Your channels with lakes collected and housed.
Since floods and swamps have free accommodation,
And tyres and Lorries are tenants and lovers,
So mud and filth are occupants and lodgers,

For the regular drone and blare of car engines,
Just like the shrieks of babies from big buses,
Is a sign that ring roads are death tracks.

Although with daggers and hoots boxers are knocked
Although their foreheads are the scene of such stabbings
Although John Sena's over-trodden body receives a million deadly blows
And Teambella, Becky and Pedge stabbed with billiards of ghastly punches
Just like Batista, Sheamus, Big Shaw, Mark Henry, and Demaize,
Their skins and foreheads look unruffled out of the boxing ring
And no trace of fierce battle is left on the ring,
Just like no trace of stabbing is left on the walls of their bodies.
A trail of Surgeons, First Aid boxes, Couches and Supporters,
 Still a stream of Management Committees flank the ring,
For sustainability aspects must ensure the lifespan of projects.
So while Government support in the form of roads
And donors intervene with capacity building
The community is the first level of sustainability
For the Council and Government must devise adapted strategies
To ensure the lifespan of roads.

Ancestral Dynasty

Along the corridors,
Along the balcony,
In all passageways,
In cues they cue,
In bliss they babble,
For the time was theirs,
And the turn was theirs.

Frenzy or Fashion?

Like a cluster of plantain stems some swerve in churches
Like a community of banana branches some waddle about
Like a bunch of palm trees they assemble in taverns,
Like a horde of tree shoots some parade streets corners
In snaky and fish-shaped cuts some swarm sea sides
Like Christmas tree some swell in tree-like garments,
In taverns and road sides they sit like shrubs.
Branches, trunks, shoots, twigs or fish;
Ravishing like fresh clothes of trees
In the wavy hands of breeze
Some do masquerade;
Naked curves and midriffs with bony carvings tattooed,
Or assortments of colours
With which they are decked,
Is the shroud that hides fading bony bodies.

Nature and Environmental Poems

※ ※

Roars and Swooshes of Menchum Falls

Thou sacred source,
Thou Holy shrine,
In whose womb is nestled
Colossal nutrients, fecund sperms and spices of black soil,
Thou sacred source,
And cradle of diversities,
On whose juicy breast Africa and grooms suck.

From the bleeding laps of African soil thou springs,
From the fertile womb of black rocks thou leaps out,
From the maternal cave of the gods thou leaps and bounces.
Like a gargle of water in the mouth;
Still like a low sonorous bubbling gurgle
From the chest of stones gushing out in resonant choirs,
Thou dart out cheerfully in two branches,
Like one in search of ancestral heritage.
Like a Christmas tree you are arrayed;
Like swimmers diving thy Twin sheets flung,
And wobbling and swaying in stately sovereignty,
Ripple roll your undulating sheets
And begin to flesh out thy sovereign colonizing course,
Like one in search of maternal home.

At the cradle of Menchum Falls;
When young rays begin to caress the pores,
And fumes of white sheets seduce my sight,
Your sonorous sighs and swooshes seduce my ears.
At the cradle of Menchum Falls;
Where like sagged breasts,
Or a droop of heavily loaded fruit tree,
The bride and bridegroom like parachutes,

Spring out from the maternity of fertile bleeding black soil.
And at the sight of the energetic Twin Parachutes;
At the sight of the hurdling and hopping waters;
Still at the sight of the spiralling and vigorous descends;
Stood we hypnotized, the Big Seeds from UBa;
Watching with awe the skydiving couple;
Vomiting into the air soaring sprays of white sheets;
Like a waterfall of menstrual flow announcing a new birth,
From the laps of African soil.
We tilted our heads and sighs and sounds we heard,
But hard was it to tell gargles from groans and roars.

At the cradle of Menchum Falls,
Where like a menstrual surge from a fecund womb
Thy waters gush out in sonorous gurgle,
The Twin Falls spring out and frog-dive in two branches,
And in widening and flaring broad,
Began the journey in search of their roots,
Or colonizing agenda as some have called it.
Surrounded by shrubs and canopies of drooping leaves,
Surrounded by giant trees and feathery leaves of palm trees,
And drooping down before our eyes, the Twin Falls
Like climbers and creepers you call mountaineers,
Stood we mesmerized, the Big Seeds,
At the womb and birthplace of blossoming Africa,
Cause in that womb is buried Africa's wealth.

Thou cradle of Africa's wealth,
Your beauty consumes my soul,
The breeze that kisses my cheeks,
And lures eyes to sleep while the mind is roused;
And like the inspired mind
Eager to forage for mental food;
A wealth of imaginative possibilities evoked.

Your veins with lavish nutrients vibrate,
The marrow in your veins is a weapon in our hands;
The vessels of your womb with fats and fuel erupt.
Like fresh palm wine dripping into a calabash,
Your nutritive womb with milk overflows.
Like fecund flow from maternal habitat
Your muscular branches with gas and oil floods,
The fuel of the country's millennium hope,
Reminiscent of your potency and virility;
For according to the Great Plan,
When thy laps menstruate, Africa is alive.

Along the banks of Menchum Falls
My ears by sounds and sighs were caressed
My ears by freezing whistling sounds were groped
My cheeks by rustling breeze were cuddled
My palms by freezing rush were hugged
My eyes by the Majestic Twin Falls were enticed
Drooping down majestically
Like heavy breasts from the walls of broad chests.

On the Majestic Twin Falls, I feasted my eyes;
The magnificent Menchum was an alluring sight.
Diving and hurdling her royal wings
Vaulting and bounding in regal leaps,
Leaping and summersaulting in ambitious rage
Like foams of furs ejaculating white sheets,
Discharging and vomiting bubbles of white,
In vaulting leaps, it tumbled and plunged.
The Stately Twin Falls was appetizing to the inner eye,
The Stately Twin Falls was my mental menu.
Her glistering waves I watched mesmerized
Its leaping ripples I watched enthralled
The voices I heard were murmurs and whispers.
The voices that raged were roars and grumbles,

Reverberating and crashing like thunderous growls.

With eyes I trailed the Majestic Menchum
In effusive frenzy its dancing waves
Like a twirl of white skirts its ripples whirled
And awakened my mind from slumber and snores.
Its sights and sounds were my mental fuel
The path it had swallowed was an attraction.

Still mesmerized I watched the pregnant waters
Still hypnotized I watched expectant waves;
In a mood of meditation I saw rising sprays;
Like rolling mountains its winding trail.
Like a snake it meandered headlong in branches;
Its waddling buttocks tantalizing tourists
Its swaying waves enticing sightseers.
Like a glutton she swallowed streams,
And after every 9 months, she hatched tributaries;
Which were all lodged in her stately waters.
Gripped and aggrieved, I watched the meandering Menchum,
On its track uprooting all intruders:
On its trail relocating all invaders,
On its trajectory evacuating trespassers;
Swamp dwellers and land grabbers I heard their screams
As Menchum meandered and swallowed invaders.

Along the banks of swelling Menchum
At the shrine of Menchum Falls
Where Christians and pagans and the categorized
Sat doubting and yawning and stretching like convicts,
To sing the praises of mystics and soothsayers.
At the shrine of Menchum Falls,
Where sat scammers in robes meant for prophets,
Where sat a trail of seers and soothsayers,
Where streams trails of prophets and astrologers,

Where floods trails of oracles and fortune-tellers,
And claim they can repair pale souls
So that from the grave
The dead will continue to sing and dance.
At the feet of seers sat cripples and the feeble,
With calabashes of palm wine and sacrificial fowls,
On the ground sat the frail and the creeping,
And on their faces lined furrows and ridges,
And their bare bodies erupting with red spots.
Eager for their turn, they stared at soothsayers,
And one after another were soaked in cool bath
For the ritual they performed at the Holy shrine,
The invisible bullets disappeared like wind.

O thou shimmering son of the Native Soil
O thou daughter of gods and goddesses,
O thou leaping and parachuting waters
O brimming eye of the gods of Wum.
The glistering amalgam of hybridized voices
Where insider and outsider trail in glee
Where gods and humans commune like one
Where ponds and streams and brooks cohabit,
Like a king and some subjected subjects,
You flesh out your course and Africa you landscaped.

Oh thou Majestic Menchum
In regal waters you meander and colonize,
Because your liberty had no borders.
Oh thou snaking and winding Menchum,
The cadences of your heart the beauty of Africa bespeaks
And contradict claims to historical barrenness.

O thou the new African river
On whose banks twirled budding buttocks
On thy course trudged fanatical tourists,

To the rhythms of your drums as you meander and roar
In cadences you rage and howl and growl,
Like the true lion of the jungle you prowl and rage.

Sustainable fountain some had clad you,
The unpolluted fecundity of black race;
Did I hear machines will invade your juicy womb?
And your inner region will be peopled by pipes?
Did I hear that in your bleeding laps;
Will be lodged aggressive pipes and pillars;
Cause The Great Plan must produce results?
Like a lad at puberty, miners feast eyes on you.
Like in-laws who storm where the sacred look with compassion;
Plumbers will plunge where divers fear to tread,
As drillers invade where mortals look with dread.
From that unholy combination energy will be born.
Through the furrows in your laps will be drained
Lakes and polls of petrol;
Like menstrual floods oil will overflow;
At every street corner lampposts will be erected;
For the potency of the womb of Menchum Falls
Will light Africa forever;
And streetlights will shine,
Where shades from forests had colonized.

Like bleeding laps your veins will bleed;
Like bleeding nose your sperm sacs will be sapped;
Like palm tree, the wine in your breasts will be tapped;
For tanks must spill with streams of lubricants;
For the Great Plan must produce upshots.
Whispers from airwaves say engines will excavate,
Your invisible wealth is what will be burrowed,
And when thy milk and semen are sapped,
And from your bosom flow fountains of fuel
And from your womb spill lakes of lubricants,

From the laps of your tributaries spring ponds of petrol
Some will call you the fertile breed,
For your womb will bleed and feed
Ships and cars and airplanes and Land rovers.
When tankers of oil will feed pipes and cables,
Where shades and shadows had threatened to engulf
Will shine like stars and moonlight and bush lamps.

When all the palm wine in the pores of your womb is exported,
And the milk in the stomata of your breasts imported,
And the fountains of fuel in the cradle of our fathers excavated,
And the juice in your veins wrenched off and extracted,
And the possessions in your sanctuary pilfered and smuggled out.
When your waters are raided by raiders,
And your sneezing laps are raped by reapers,
And your virginity defiled by pipes and pillars,
And like a frowning mask your womb wear ridges and furrows;
Like butchered beef your sacred region will be slaughtered.
When in the process of excavating your womb is excavated,
When in the process of quarrying an abortion is caused,
Because pipes must forage for fuel;
While to miners you look appetizing,
To versifiers and ecologists you'll look unappetizing,
And like a disvirgined lad you'll appear unenticing.

O thou stately Twin Falls,
When your dominion will be invaded,
And in your womb is lodged raging machines,
And in the embrace of your arms is wedged Dams and pipelines,
The vessels in your brain will be ruptured,
And like a malformed foetus,
The limbs of your tributaries will tilt and deviate on one side.
When the air above your heads suffocates with gruesome smoke,
That surge out from your butchered womb,
Leaves will wither and fade like shreds,

While shrubs and flowers will develop red scabies.

O Menchum Twin Falls, the hope of Africa,
The fecund and untainted abode of the divinities,
Like palm tree from which calabashes scoop out virgin palm wine,
Like a waterfall of menses guarantees a buzzing baby hatchery,
Your nutrients and diving waters lure tourists and investors,
But when pipes burrow through and rape your virgin laps,
And tap from its well cradled breasts all the juicy marrow,
When your womb will shrink and shrivel;
And the milk in the breast of your soil
Is mauled for marrow by gluttons and tappers,
When you are no more,
Africa and her groom will mourn more and more.

Garments of Nature and Clothes of Trees

Cuddling shivering clothes of trees bathed in beads of sweat,
During such moments when the sky has urinated;
And the soaked leaves shed tears in silence;
With the sky's urine shrubs and I were soaked,
And trembling like the feverish leaves I stood.
Clothes of trees shedding tears I saw;
Across bamboo trees with feathery leaves I peered,
Across intertwined shrubs and tufts of palm fronds I trudged;
Across ravishing green curls of creeping foliage I spiraled,
On the fluffy foliage I foraged and scavenged,
On buds and blooms my gluttonous eyes feasted,
On sprouts and shoots my greedy senses harvested,
As nodding palm trees nod to soaring assertive trunks,
In search of mental diet I rummaged.

For when the mind awakened from slumber is stirred,
The fertile thoughts in pictures are employed
That tale can only moods and feelings tell better,
For no lips such wealth of nature can bore.
Immediately my sterile thoughts were nurtured,
Immediately my senses were roused;
Like excited veins drugged with marijuana,
Pictures appeared though no eyes could see,
The sonorous lyrics drizzling from beaks I listened,
The breeze on its wingless flight I felt,
The fluttering birds on ruffled foliage I perceived,
And as my wits on nature's wealth slurped and dined,
And my senses on nature's coats and breasts of green sucked and drunk;
So my mind with nature's wealth was nourished.

Roasting Air and Raiding Winds of Filthy Estate

Trudging along butchered streets in the heart of Africa,
Plodding through slaughtered tars in the soul of the city,
Lurking like shadows of street children across gaping tars,
Plodding like rattling tires through pools of ponds,
Waddling like ducks in gaping ponds colonizing wounded tars,
Wobbling through trails of stagnant traffic flow,
Greeted by smothering smoky air invading my eyes and nasals,
And squatting extensions scuttling into hearts of roads I saw.

Drenched bodies erupting with bites of mosquitoes,
On every face noddle-like bumps and burrs from bites of mosquitoes,
Flesh around the arms burrowed through by meandering millipedes,
Drenched faces streaming with pools of blazing sweat,
Crumpled nostrils invaded by harassing claws of heat,
Furrowed foreheads assaulted by biting breeze,
Butchered water pipes farting and urinating purring urine,
Rapping my flesh was the sweltering heat,
Tapping my flesh was oppressive air,
Pecking my legs was some tyrannical breeze
Swishing through the air spaces of the city,
Nibbled by choking purr of farts from anuses of gnarled cars,
And trailing the swerve of giant timbers roofing lorry tops.

Trudging along butchered gaping streets in the heart of the city,
Plodding through slaughtered muddy streets in the soul of the city,
Strolling along dead streets in the bosom of the city,
The things I felt and the sight I saw;
Roof tops of factories vomiting into the air trails of dark smoke,
Windows of factories bleeding out thick sheets of brown smoke,
Roof tops of locomotives spitting into the air dark brown lanes of
smoke,

Anal cavities of vehicles excreting into the air thick shrouds of smoke,
Every roadside I saw were lined with ridges of rubbish,
Every roadside I saw had tiny mountains of filth,
Stagnant-slimy-creamy-brown-coloured waters,
In whose embrace is nestled tufts of swarming germs.
Swarms of flies taking off and landing on swollen heaps of stinking garbage,
Clusters of mosquitoes hovering and scavenging on slimy creams of invasive morsels,
Throngs of beetles excavating and feasting on wounded heaps of excrement,
Bony hands of hawkers foraging for bottles and plastics in tiny mountains of garbage heaps,
Snakes and gigantic rats foraging and rummaging through fragments of toxic waste,
Twirls of oppressive heat gushing out of the laps of rubbish heaps,
Bustles of gnawing smoke invading my eyes and causing eye bleeding,
Surges of roasting smoke invading my nasals and causing nose bleeding,
Gnarled smoke spiralled up from roadside firesides;
And every road user I met their nostrils with fingers were cupped,
Every passer-by I met their chests were rising and falling as they coughed and panted,
For the air we sniffed our lungs were strangled,
For the smoke we inhaled our lungs were assaulted,
Just like the sight we watched our eyes were invaded.

Lumbering across the hairy palm bushes of the Grassfields
Trudging across the bearded shrubs of the rice fields,
Swishing through the whispering forests of the Savannah,
The things I felt and the sight I saw;
Jackets of dust on every leaf,
Misery and frowns on crinkled leaves,
Fear and drench and on wrinkled leaves,
Hunger and pain on puckered faces of flowers,
Burns and blisters on rumpled banana leaves,

Shivering like patients were pale leaves,
Bony and exposed were fleshless roots of tree trunks,
Looking starved were dry bones of mango branches,
Starved of rain, the passing wind and sunlight was maize and cassava
sprouts,
Buried in the soil were infected tins and papers,
And that soil was raped and her hymen destroyed.

As I slept and fantasized a dream I had,
Pollution could be history,
If refuse in trash cans are put,
If roadsides be not littered,
If factories away from towns could be lodged,
If our cars like grafted fruits be made greener,
And if our soils are spared by rapists like tins and papers.

National Integration, Patriotism, Peace Building, Democratic Practice, Political and Historical Poems

Religious Democracy

Religious democracy breeds prostitution,
Its drainages floods with migrants, immigrants and nomads.
Because non-achievers and Ex-convicts are proprietors of churches;
While their wives and children are church Accountants and Bankers.
While for the proprietors of these commercial enterprises
Evangelization is less traumatic and juicy business
For conscience and moral law, the sheep is fed with filth.

Kitchens and bedrooms host temples and churches;
Like commercial enterprises churches swell with contractors,
While the Gospel is advertised, commercialized and sold
And Holy creeds marketed, wholesaled, and retailed
Sacraments are hawked, traded and vended;
And like Sexually Transmissible Marks
Miracles are drainage strategies.

While miracles are the tools of this flourishing business;
With religious earthquakes the earth is feverish;
For the anointed water just like anointed oil,
Is hawked at cutthroat prices to poor parishioners.
While the Disciples of miracles call others "comfort zones";
They spent the first mass in the Anointed Church,
While the second mass takes place in cults and shrines.

The Birth of the Great Triangle

When in the warm embrace of our virgin arms
We strangled nests of thorns with vibrant laughter,
Like an imbedded plant was our virgin narrative grafted,
And out of that intercourse was hatched a great Triangle,
And in the heart of the great Triangle, our two eager souls forever
wedded.
Dear spiders of tales of birth and heritage,
Into excavation sites throng and dig,
Spin not thy yarn into traps of thread,
Spin into chaste yarn your tale of heritage.
From the raffia fiber plucked and plaited by the grey hair brain,
Will the product of its fertility clock weave its own garment.

The Raging 90s

The past is still alive. The scars are still visible.
Remember Snake
Remember the hurricane howling across trees and bedrooms.
Remember how verbal debris ripped through roofs of hearts,
Remember the price we paid.
Remember how we chased and were traced.
Remember how the trapper was trapped in his trap.
Remember lives wedged in flames.
Remember lives hemmed in mud.
Remember the legs thunder past; shaking hearts and houses.
Remember the bullets hovering, roaring, hooting, charging and beeping.
Remember the swarm of bullets that left gaping holes on the walls
of chests.
Remember how bullets stormed and dislodged hearts from blossom-
ing bodies.
Remember the blasts whistling, shrieking and screeching.
Remember the shuts prattling, jabbering, gibbering and galloping.
Remember the bows flaring, tracing, storming and stabbing.
Remember the bangs babbling, gyrating and rambling.
Remember the bumps shouting and shattering; rioting and raging.
Remember the arrows slaughtering, crashing and crushing.
Remember the spears piercing, assaulting, penetrating and invading.
Remember the babbling and chattering above our hands and heads.
Remember the punches and strokes.
Remember the thumps, the whacks and smacks.
Remember the cries and screams and shouts and shrieks.
Remember how in matted forests, we crept and crawled around.
Remember how we trailed with rats and maggots.
Remember how furrowed faces peeked over collapsing walls to see
the outside world.
Remember how eyes wept to see fruits of the womb wedged in flames.

Remember the buildings crumbling and swallowing staggering legs.
Remember how faces crumpled with pain.
Remember how we clutched and leaped on clutches.
Remember how hawks hunched and plunged into budding laps.
Remember how we hopped and dropped in matted bushes.
Remember how legs rustled through bushes.
Remember the damages. Remember the boredom.
Remember the spears wedged between chest bones.
Remember colonies of flies feasting on remains of children who should
live to testify that we were fathers and not just men.
Remember the voices screaming under beds in pains of childbirth.
Remember the fowls and goats we lost to thieves who wasted no time
to take advantage of the unfortunate incident.
Remember intestines grumbling and howling.
Remember how we devour leaves and barks of trees.
Remember the long lines in bakeries.
Remember how we yawned and stretched.
Remember the number of years Ability and hunters spent in
Cavendengue.
Remember how their children abandoned the classroom for abandoned
vehicles.
Remember Ngunso and Din. Remember Gali and Gawoh.
Remember Havory Coat, Dybia, Generia and Bukarama,
Remember Konga, Vulnesia, Jijip and Tuturu Wakamuru,
Remember Nkolofata, Futocol and Mayo Danei,
Remember Din, Yeeh, Balikumbat and Bambalang
Remember budding souls slaughtered, roasted, smoked and baked.
Remember the lifeless heads yawning and gawking.
Remember uncountable-unidentified headless trunks.
Remember that a hero does not crash without relics of the crash.

The Plaited-Ropes

Clad in rags of heritage and bearded history,
Clothed in garments of heritage and hairy history,
Married at menopause and yet was still fertile,
Was a plaited name which like the length of a river,
Or even the endless trails of bush fire smoke
 Creeping over the shoulders of the walls of the sky in curls,
Stretching across the thick thickets of the bearded continent
And is now engraved on the canon like Africa's date of birth;
A name every strand of family attachment bears,
A name branches and leaves of the Great trunk bear,
A name into Mother Earth like deep taproots planted.

Clad in rags of heritage and bearded history,
Clothed in garments of heritage and hairy history;
Sprouting up and blooming out like potent seeds,
Was the plaited tale of a family tree;
A great trunk whose tap roots like an umbilical cord
Into African soil were deeply planted.
And the umbilical cord of that heritage,
Just like the relics and attractions of that family tree;
Which ink continue to graft and weave,
Was the tale from whose womb sprung out twins and triplets.

Sprouting up from a potent and muscular trunk,
In suckers and clusters like a heavy bunch of banana
Sitting on the neck of a banana stem;
Clustered plaited ropes melded into one bunch to divorce no more,
For wedlock is the currency with which peace is bought.
And the wedding germinated like a ripening lad,
About to be hauled to a domestic colonizer,
Because tradition says she was born before her time.

Clothed in a mosaic of branches and clusters
Like triplet tributaries from the same source
Mining milk from the chest of the Great River,
Was the origin of the grafted tale, into one great rope plaited,
Like many threads of the same rope woven;
Because many side shoots of the same trunk interwoven,
Into hybrid branches springing up and propagating,
Just like grafted fruits overhanging like foliage,
Were triplet embryos in the same womb incubating.

Weaned from the breasts of darkness they claimed,
Like a betrothed lad uprooted from her mother's breast
By virtue of their numeric strength in the ornamented alliance
The wedding was solemnized with the Bible as witness.
While for white-bearded history it was salad cream in one dish blended,
And for God Mother it was light and darkness in one conviction wedded,
For sons of the native soil it was a festooned and polygamous communion.

While for the matrilineal side shoot of the plaited tale,
Bride price was never paid on the bride as custom demanded;
And for the patrilineal branch, it was libation on a polygamous monogamy celebrated;
For social gate keepers the wedding was solemnized without libation;
Whereas for in-laws and indigenes it was "Unity in diversity";
For hoisted history whose crash was dramatic,
The name of the plaited twin tale was polyandry.

Clothed in a mosaic of clusters and suckers,
Like triplet tributaries from the same source sucking,
Was the plaited name of a great trunk;
A name every strand of family roots bears,
A name whose crossbreed vocabulary bears,

A name tributaries and branches of the Great family bear,
Because in that crossbreed name was their umbilical cord buried,
Because in that hybrid name was their crashed history born,
And in that hybridized name their fallen tradition resurrected.

Just like a felled tree whose half-metre dead trunk
 Revives and begins to bear side shoots again;
Or even like Christ who died and was resurrected,
So must the grafted tale be revived to survive;
So must dismantled maps be re-erected;
So must the deposed fireside stories be disentombed;
So must unseated history which we recall in pain be enthroned.

For that tale to metamorphose into a cultural residue,
For the cultural residue to become a communal reservoir,
For the communal reservoir to be engraved on the cultural desert,
For the cultural desert to have another red feather quivering on its cap,
As recognition for stretching the line of brain children
Hatched in Africa's academic maternity;
And for raising the cultural residue to the rank of a heroic canon,
African writers must to excavation sites throng;
African writers must to shrines and alters storm;
And through prayers, offerings and incantations exhume or perform:
Song and sounds, images and emblems,
Rites and rituals, riddles and proverbs,
Folklore and artefacts, dance and libations,
Myths and legends, heroes and heroines,
 Masks and shrines, sculptures and statues;
Mortars and drums, and palm branches and herbs;
For in such excavation sites lies Africa's nerve and soul;
For in such archaeological sites lies the cure of Africa's nervous erosion,
For in such excavation sites lies the cure for Africa's bareness and
nakedness;

For only through literary excavations
Can we be able to restore our eroded dignity,
And proactively resuscitate the crashing relics of African fellowship
/brotherhood.

Grafted Fruits and Borrowed Feathers

Clothed in rags of heritage and bearded history,
Arrayed in rags of hoary and plaited history,
Like a cobweb of connections or a bunch of banana
Flocked we in the second home which was carved out for us by
Motherland,
Strapped onto the walls of the back and chest to tap from the Catch-
ment tank.

Like sapped up veins in need of blood-donors we looked thirsty and
withered.
Droning like a cluster of bees snoring in the beehive were blood donors
with blood bags,
Buzzing in sonorous gurgles like streams gushing out of rocky cavities
And from the foot of the mountainous Motherland where sat we like
beggars
A lullaby we heard drizzling in our ears:
"Darkness had bathe the land in shades",
"The land was barren and needed dung",
"The sun will shine where shadows had engulfed".

As entangling and interweaving was the sweet cradle song,
In the warm embrace of our arms we embraced the dung donors,
And like a butterfly that sheds off its hard shell,
And in thoroughly embellished garments scrambled,
To soar above every other head like hanging-shoulders birds,
The half-bloods were decked out in borrowed feathers.
Through the wedding we became polluted species of crossbreeds
Forgetting that our true origin was the creeping caterpillar.

Unknown to us our ways were shredded to crumbs,
Unknown to us the river it was that fed on its tributaries,

For though crawling under the weight of the Elephant
Were Anthills and dung donors,
Yet still groping into holes with toe nails
For crickets and beetles were Anthills and dung donors.

In the second home a dominion they carved out,
Like plaited ropes its inhabitants were new breeds of hybrids
And cross-pollinated species and crossbreeds;
Like the painted walls of a mended building
The second home was a breeding ground
For blood pollution and embedded breeds.

The Report Card of Democracy

Like mass exodus of refugees and migrants,
Verbal diarrhoea spring out from lips,
Newspapers pour in on all sides
Like mass migration of honey bees
Because the New Deal says it is time to talk.
Women and their art gain grounds and more visibility;
Like the Civil Society, Medias vomit debris on air waves,
Although Rigour and Moralization frown on abuses and says:
"Be not injurious and destructive in the execution of democratic rights."

Political parties crop up in slums and ghettos;
Religious shrines spring up in bedrooms
Freedom of opinion floods in lips and books
With no speed breaks as to what can be said;
(Excerpt where insolence is understood as democracy)
The masses lay legitimate demands on Command,
While Big guns shiver and grunt and gnash teeth in cages,
Because the New Deal says democracy is not immunity.

Social Clinic

In search of healing herbs and curative reeds,
In search of what cools off the tempest of anger;
In search of what cools off the flames of conflict;
Because where the seeds of conflict sprouts
Poverty and hunger incubates and flowers.
In search of what quenches the fury of the race for inheritance,
In search of what causes the storm of hunger for power to abate;
In search of what can extinguish the tempests of terrorism;
Because where the seeds of conflict take roots
Tolerance and acceptance wither and fade like overused garments.
In search of what tames an injurious tongue
For the flair of unhealthy emotions is barbaric and ravaging;
Social mediation and indigenous response options are
Pedagogues and healing herbs.

In quest of what extinguishes the rage of land disputes;
In search of what stubs out the flair of farmer-grazier conflicts
In search of what prunes off the roasting heat of conflict of authority
In search of what crops off the sweltering drought of poverty
In search of what trims off the oppressive fangs of terrorism
In search of what snips off the blazes of unhealthy human emotions
Dialogue, the family, the Priest, the Pastor and the Imam
Just like understanding, Social Welfare and legal redress
Are diagnostic and healing herbs.

In search of what drowses the stings and glares of hatred and envy;
In search of what inundates and drains the scorching fangs of nepotism
In quest of solutions to the savagery of polygamy and domestic violence
In search of the way out of the flurry and fires of religious Tremors
and earthquakes;
In search of how to quench the ravaging flames of power tussle;

In search of how to cause the extinction of the stench of greed and
pride,
Because morals are in a state of comma;
In search of a coffin in which to seal individualistic sentiments;
In search of a casket as big as the size of jealousy;
In search of what can cultivate peace,
And stem the tides of Human Rights Abuses;
For words can fuel or cool off tempests;
Plant and water the seeds of peace to sprout and flower.

Dear anthems of intolerance and divide:
Dialogue hatches heroes and heroines
Tolerance gives birth to victory
Respect for the trunk and branches guarantees unity
Negotiation cures eruptions and explosions
Mending or grafting humbles violence
And recognition of others breeds social integration.

Compose no more anthems of divide:
Love like tolerance silences guns and upsurges,
Coupling in diversity is the taproots of undying strength
Religious and Ethnic acceptance engender love
Humility defeats pride in its own field of play,
And programmes the burial of epidemics and tempests,
For creeds must be medicinal, regenerative and restorative.

Dear political, religious and traditional players;
Toxic consciousness infects dreams
Nepotism slaughters job descriptions
Unpatriotic lyrics assassinate projects
Songs of divide slay big ambitions
But one culture, one song and one people is therapeutic
For socio-trans/National integration heals
But divide plants the deadly seeds of hatred;
And renders develoPMent epileptic and galloping.

Dear political and traditional players;
When freedom becomes a scare commodity
A soothing tongue can tame and repair and mould.
Be no more hawkers of rumbling and raging storms,
Enrol your tongue and unhealthy emotions
In the Higher Institute of Conscience, Ethics and Morality.

Vaccine against Violence

Violence does stings,
Violence never heals,
And when violence stings,
Because a sting does kills,
And the killed does stinks;
The nation in size shrinks,
And family dreams do sink;
And never shall the family sing,
For buried are budding skills.

So in order not to shrivel and shrink;
For like mushrooms must our Anthem spring,
And like young nipples must the Map bustle and brim;
The rage of verse should replace the rattles of bombs and bullets,
While the threads of negotiation should weave and plait,
And mould and tame and graft and patch and repair.

Abuja June, 2016

The Wedding

From aborted engagement to patched up polyandry,
From turbulent polygamy to grafted monogamy,
From an adopted child to a biological child,
From foster fathers to biological fathers
From betrothal without libation to libation at menopause;
So the betrothed in the womb from arm to arm prostituted;
And like a ravishing lad at puberty whose beauty
Is a feast for the wandering greedy eyes of eye robbers;
The bride was a blooming hunting ground
For inheritors and roaming land grabbers.

From one alliance to another alliance,
From one courtship to another courtship,
And from the staggering sixty to a settled sixty one,
A communal ritual ended all unholy alliances;
What in the eyes of indigenous suitors was forced marriages,
Although the end of the alliance was the birth of a new marriage.
Like a house that on a solid rock was constructed
So that the house will survive in times of storm,
So on a solid foundation was the marriage constructed.
Like an *obanje* child whose death is the beginning of reincarnation,
So was our wedding day our birth day.

Our date of birth was the wedding day we all adored
A day in the courtroom stood the couple and witnesses well adorned,
A day in the courtroom were fingers with bridal rings well festooned,
A day in the courtroom a monogamous fellowship well engraved.
A day the families of bride and groom like a millipede who has one thousand legs
And moves with all his one thousand legs into the courtroom stormed;
A day like the teeth and the tongue into the same room we were lodged.

A day the only song we sang was unity in diversity
A day like the tree and its roots we united in diversity
A day when our uneasy dreams and strategies took roots
A day our differences like palm oil and water in one pot dissolved;
A day our hates and sorrows in one grave buried
A day our diversities our source of strength became.

Through the marriage ring our two souls in one home were roommates,
Through the marriage pledge our two voices in one voice covenanted,
Through the marriage oath our two homes in one room lodged
Through the marriage vows our two eyes in one mirror cotenanted,
Through the marriage ring our two languages in the same mouth cohabited
Through the marriage ring our two languages like husband and wife
In the same bed lay side by side;
Through the marriage ring our giant ambitions and vast projects like a plant took roots.

In the presence of Motherland and Fatherland as witnesses,
In the presence of creators and in-laws as witnesses,
 On our marriage Certificates these words were inscribed:
Joint property was the oath we took,
Co-authorship was the vow we took,
Co-custody was the promise we made,
Like husband and wife, English and French together will horde,
Under rain or sun like soldier ants and termites together we troop,
In happiness or sadness, in poverty or riches together we flock,
In times of storm, together we resist was the pledge we made;
In times of war like a bunch of banana forever we bunch,
Never to divorce twice was the undertaking we signed;
Forever like sheep we flock was the attitude we entertained,
In times of penury together we starve was the vow we contracted;
Our National Rituals under the same foliage observed was the option we chose,
In times of harvest together we fellowship was the opinion we

embraced;
Our collective consciousness in two linguistic vehicles traced was the
vision envisaged,
Our expiation rites in the same shrine conducted was the vow we
engaged,
Our vote cast into one ballot box dropped was the option we hugged,
Our rites and rituals in the same shrine performed was the idea we
kissed,
Our common rituals in the same stage performed was the option we
nestled;
To shield each other like Lions and Gorillas was the choice we nurtured,
And the choices we made were the foundation of our future,
For the choices we make will make or mar.

Determined to trek on grounds where first generation suitors and
in-laws
And great grandfathers refused to trudge;
Determined to pay a posthumous bride price
The first generation in-laws did not relish;
So that in retrospect we can be cleansed where we erred;
Through the marriage of offspring, a posthumous libation was poured;
And by the terms of that matrimony a posthumous bride price And
libation at menopause was the ritual conducted;
And to the abode of the divinities the new bride and groom were led,
And in that holy cradle palm wine into a calabash cup was poured,
And as the bride and groom from the same cup in turns drank,
From the lips of the High Priest drizzled the following words:

Gods of our land,
Rocks of black soil,
Legs of Elephants,
Pillars of our land,
Eyes and ears of the black race;
Warriors who never miss target when they shoot;
Shields of orphans;

Kifir, new moon, five suns and ten rains in the year of locusts,
We bring our children Esther and Guillaume to the alter,
To be bonded as husband and wife;
They are now like a house
Which like the trunk of a tree
Must their roots deep into the soil be firmly planted;
May the union we struggle to build
In sweat and toil never into shreds be shredded;
May the union we struggle to construct never into pieces crash;
May the abode of children for which fertility is implored
Ten branches of trees with fruits be born;
May in the marriage two cultures marry,
May in the marriage two languages marry,
May in the marriage two families marry,
From you we seek fertility
From you we seek security
To you we pledge loyalty
From you we seek national integration.

May you accept the palm wine and the goat
May you to us grant your protective potent
We beg for your shield,
Where we erred grant us cleansing;
May we through the marriage
One voice, one graft, one humanity, one roof.

The journey may be long and windy
Its tracks curvy and thorny
But like a game of football
Or a stage performance
Where all players like all actors
Are important for the plot to end in a comedy;
May plot and sub-chapters of joyous sorrows end in a comedy;
We can realize the dream if the will is there.

Defend the Flag

Where the Flag is hoisted is the heart of the Nation,
Where the heart of the Nation is erected is our umbilical cord;
Where our umbilical cord is lodged is our collective consciousness.
In that sacred soil the Nation's heart-beats is our progress clock,
In that blessed soil the heart of the Nation is what we married,
In that sanctified soil the ears of the Nation are always alert,
In that consecrated soil the mind of the Nation is always dreaming
And in that deified soil is our enduring values.

In the heart of the Nation the future is planted
And the colours of that green plant are "Green, Red, Yellow";
In the heart of the nation is the cradle of our heritage;
On the top of the canopy I find a beacon
In the heart of the beacon is the past and future of our great Nation
planted and reared;
So;
Defend the Flag
Shield the land,
And calm the storms of antagonistic dogmas,
Never in history must our heritage into shreds be rendered.

In the heart of the nation
Must peace be planted
In the soul of the nation
Must unity be planted.
In the heart of the nation
Must love be planted
In the trunk of the nation
Must gaping holes never be seen.
For in one voice never will territorial integrity be dismantled,
For in one voice never will state dignity be humbled.

Defend the Flag
Shield the land
And calm the storms of divide.
For the walls of the nation
Must never be ripped to rags
For the walls of the nation
Must never tremble and crumble.

Shield the Flag
The roof over your heads;
For the walls of the nation
Must never know eruptions
For the walls of the nation
Must never crash and collapse.
For in one voice never will territorial integrity crumble,
For in one voice never will state dignity be humbled.

Clad the Flag
With robs of love
Shield the Flag
With libation and prayers.
From the eyes of the nation
Must never know tears
For the eyes of the nation
Must tears never flow.
For in one voice will territorial integrity never crumble,
For in one voice will state dignity never be humbled.

Defend the Flag
Guard the Flag
And calm the storms of greed.
By the strength of salt and palm wine will we forever be coupled,
For in one song will cultural boundaries be amputated,
For under one thinking cap will gender barriers be butchered,
For in one anthem will ethnic barriers be banished.

For in one voice will racial barriers be battered,
For in one nod will hate preaching be banned.
For in one voice will class distinction be fractured,
For in one dream will diversity be our source of strength.
Hatch no more anthems of divide,
Hatch and hum melodies of grafting and mending.

Cameroon

The umbilical cord of a Great family tree;
The cradle of conjoined rivers,
Whose conjoined twin-birth
Gushed out from the laps of history,
Like the hybrid progenies of the West Indies;
And became in the eyes of both bride and groom,
A conjoined inheritance woven into a pregnant triangle,
With the tissues and threads of history.

Was conceived in the matrimonial bed of history,
Born by history and re-created by plaited history;
And nestled in a thatched palm-frond bed,
Woven into crossbreed-wavy raffia fibres,
And reared in the fence of the Great Triangle,
With pure palm wine from the fecund
Black soils of prenatal history.

Dear monument of martyrs and saviours,
The fibre from which East and West,
Like a twin-birth, are into one woven;
For in your matted umbilical cord, are two souls blended,
And in that wedding ring, in cohesion, we are plaited,
Clustering with suckers like a sugar cane trunk;
Bunching together like a bunch of plantains;
And trudging together like a millipede and its thousand legs.

Driven at bearded stage, by productivity;
And driven by the dream to metamorphose and improve;
For a steady hand must be kept on the steering wheel;
She became a treasured athlete in the global race of hope.
And at the stage when age, like a ripe banana,

Or young-green-orange shoots spring up
From the limbs of chests of climbers,
Beloved Cameroon was betrothed to history by history;
A wedding solemnized by Francois and Belter,
In an oath whose terms were:
'For better or for worse,
In sickness and in health,
In poverty and in plenty,
Till death do us part'.

As the path to the summit was rough and muddy,
Just like the race of hope was ran on rocky slopes;
A hand of friendship, she extended;
The hand of partnership was alluring,
And the roots and tentacles of cooperation she stretched;
For in a game of football, teamwork is communion,
For technology and expertise must in size grow;
For with technology, intelligence and collaboration, will we emerge.

Beloved Cameroon,
The one and indivisible umbilical cord,
The river whose tributaries from same birthplace traced;
In your relics and symbols is our collective psyche;
In your artefacts and footages is our communal soul;
In your myths and memorials is our plaited heritage lodged;
A heritage bought with blood and tears;
For their sun rose and set in streams of blood,
For the road they trudged was full of thorns.

Dear monuments of the native soil;
Through whose dream we are strewn;
You can smile and nod as you keep guard,
For in unison our drums and voices sing and dance.
Dear immortal martyrs of black soil,
Whose voices, past and present, I still hear:

Manga Bell, Um Nyobe, Moumie, Ouandie, Marie Mbida,
Foncha, Endeley, Muna, Atangana, Ahidjo, and Biya!
Before you I bring a calabash of palm-wine,
To feed our gods as you pronounce:
'May the bloodstreams of their veins never be gripped by disease,
May the tubers and lungs of their throats never be raped of breath'.

Dear Motherland;
The plough of the coastal banana plantations,
The rider on whose back we ride,
The fulcrum of the nation's develoPMent dreams,
The wheels and wings of our ever glowing dreams,
The storehouse of Makossa, Bikutsi, and Bensikin,
Including Njang, sighs, whispers, and raging hums and rhythms
Of the coastal and Grassfield tribes;
The breadbasket of Africa and foreign spouses,
Secured through trade and mutual partnership weddings,
And also through administrative and academic marriages.

Dear ancestral land,
In whose womb are wedded 'bonjour' and 'good morning';
You are a promising land of splendour,
You are a fertile womb of majestic excavation sites,
And a sterilized sanctuary of myths and symbols,
For in your universe of diversities,
Which is the repository of a bi-heritage,
And which holds together,
The soul of our forward trudging nation,
As a community of shared heritage;
In you, just like husband and wife,
Is a cohabitation of sounds and sighs;
Of arts objects and myths
Of sands and sights;
Of Falls and forests,
Of quarries and Games,

Of Monkeys and Gorillas,
Of mortars and immortals,
And blend of natives and displaced and the stray and refugees.

Dear great Mother,
In whose womb, and for nine painful months
We were lodged rent-free;
Our soils and skins are exposed to stabbing stings,
And to assaults from dust-laden harmattan winds,
And need conservation and preservation;
For you remain the shelter, the refuge, and the asylum camp.

Oh great Mother,
In whose treasured archive we live like a couple,
Be the colonizer and not the colonized,
Be the conqueror and not the conquered,
For poverty and disease must shrink in size,
For savagery and propaganda must be crushed to death;
If we must survive the dead blows of incursions.

O great Mother;
Be the landlord in your own home,
And not a tenant in your own home.
Be the author in your vocab,
And not the parody in your vocab.
Be the main plot in your tale,
And not the sub-plot of your tale.
Be a son of the native soil in your homeland,
And not a stranger in your homeland.
Be the stream that feeds its tributaries,
And not a tributary in your own river.
Be the owner of your own roof,
And not a tenant under your roof.
Be the staff that directs the blind,
And not the blind guided by the staff.

Be the heir to your father's throne,
And not a foster son to your father's throne.
Be the trunk of your own tree,
And not the branches of your tree.
Be the trunk in your territory,
And not the clusters in your territory.
Be the lion in your den,
And not the lion without a den.

Be a king in your kingdom,
And not a titled man without a tribal constituency.
Be the Emperor in your Empire,
And not the Emperor without an Empire.
Be the hunter in your dominion,
And not the hunted in your dominion.
Be couch and player in your team,
And not a player in your team.

O Great Mother,
Out of the bloodstreams of the nation,
Must life never be scooped out,
Out of the veins of the land,
Must nutrients never shrivel,
For the pores of the land,
Must never know dehydration.
Out of the lungs of the land,
Must breathe never dry off,
For the roots must not create a farm
In another plantation.
May the droppings of our dreams,
Manure the ambitions of our souls.

Healing Herbs

When conflict becomes volcanic,
Because when tension erupted,
And emotions were raging,
While anger became chronic,
Unsettled disputes gave birth to storms,
For conflict accumulated causes heart –bleeding;
From eyes and hearts bleed out waterfalls of tears.

When dialogue is protracted,
And disputes grow like mountains,
Hatred and jealousy tear through hearts,
While intolerance rears savagery and barbarism,
And fuel the flames of aggression;
And cause the fury of feelings to explode.

When conflict becomes volcanic,
With its flames the heart consuming,
And its ears like blasts rattling,
And its lips every word stabbing and tearing,
And its fangs into every flesh gnawing,
And peace into shreds rending,
And the air we breathe polluted,
And the liberty we wield assaulted,
And the young we should tame made savages,
Because money became their lures,
Peace and security into shreds are reduced.

On how to heal the storms of disagreement,
Because early solutions can quench off the flames of conflict;
On how to concoct a marriage of shadow and light,
For early decision-making spruce-off the pollution of bitterness;

On how to make fertile marriage at menopause,
For alternatives and negotiation reduce the earthquakes of the heart;
On how to mend broken homes and hearts,
For sharing of feelings and ideas is the cure for chronic conflict;
On the dining table must all in a cluster sit:
Preachers, Traditional Rulers, Kings,
The dissidents, the State, and world Bodies,
From the same dish must we all dine,
And the anthems of oaths must be sang,
For the roots of the rage must we excavate.

With the ears must we listen,
With the lips must we heal,
In the coffin must guns be buried,
With dialogue must the fury of conflict be quenched,
With negotiation must the taunts of words be extinguished,
With apologies must the scotch of verbal terrorism be stubbed out,
With explanation must the flames of anger be drenched,
With the heart must we forgive,
And with the arms must we each other embrace.

And now to hardliners,
On a scale must damage and peace be measured,
On a balance must results and consequences be graded;
Like a grafted tree must palm oil and water be wedded;
Just like the teeth and tongue in one room reside,
So like a couple must humanity and religions in one room be nestled.
And now to hardliners;
Sting with words and heal with words,
For healing stings are better than nests of thorns.

Tolerance

As we set sail into the unknown waters of 2016
Tolerance is the only balm;
The store house of peace,
The millipede which has one thousand children
But takes all along wherever it goes;
The family head who has all categories of children including the mad ones,
But accepts all;
The best robe that can cloth us;
The only cure that can cause the storm of violent fanaticism to abate,
Or makes the magma of the mind to subside;
The preferred herb that heals toxic ideologies;
The undying music whose melodious tone subdues hardened hearts;
The only language that transforms rebels into loyal subjects
Or cause foes to become friends;
The only discourse that frowns at sentiments of divide,
And cause the East to cohabit with the West,
Or cause black skins to dine with white skins;
The only subject that teaches love and acceptance;
The only pedagogic lectures whose message is "respect for hierarchy";
The moral guide whose vision is respect for state institutions;
The only poem whose imagery warns against environmental degradation;
The only play text that dramatizes the fruits of patriotism;
The only novel whose narrative hinges on One Nation, One Voice, One People.

緋緋

Social Menu

In the garden of morals,
Ethics are planted,
And when harvest time comes,
Peace is cultivated.

In the orchard of religious diversity,
The sperms of tolerance are planted,
And when harvest time is near,
Peace and security are cultivated.

In the fertile womb of Cameroon soils,
The seeds of patriotism are incubated,
And when harvest time is ripe,
Peace and Security are garnered.

In the fecund fields of Millennium Dreams,
The spirit of Hard Work is cultivated,
And when Harvest time rears its head,
Emergence will be reaped.

In the virile Agricultural Estate of Democracy,
Good choices are planted,
And when harvest time announces itself,
Results and not consequences are hoisted.

In the Estate of DeveloPMent Dreams,
Goals and methods are engendered,
And when harvest time springs up,
Results are erected.

In the fertile New Deal Garden,

Democracy is planted,
And when harvest time rings its bells,
Religious shrines and Multipartism mushroom in bedrooms.

In the garden of Good Governance,
Tasks are guided by terms of reference,
And when the fever of failure threatens,
The cures of failure flowers like sprouts of teenage climbers.

So prepare the nursery,
Dig deep into subsoil like taproots,
And in the garden of life plant edible seeds,
For when harvest time is ripe, what you sow is what you reap.

❦ ❦

The Broom

Sweep well broom,
And clear the way for bride and groom,
Sweep well broom,
And from the heart of Africa flush out gloom.

Sweep well broom,
And clear the mess that litters the bedroom,
Filter well broom,
For the river like streams is murky and muddled.

Cleanse well broom,
For the heart of the church house is filthy and brown.
Rinse well broom,
For the hands of Finance are soiled and muddy.

Sweep well cleaners,
For the dust you raise will blind your eyes.
Judge well critics,
For the standards you set will be your traps.

Heal well herbs,
For alcohol in intestines is fermented and infected.
Purify well surgeon,
For blood in the liver is polluted and contaminated.

Heal well dogmas
For the soul of humans is infected with greed,
Heal well creeds
For thoughts and wishes are toxic like tobacco.

Teach well pedagogues
For the emotions of the twenties are poisonous like pollution,
Teach well pedagogues
For ambitions of the twenties are enormous and venomous.

Bathe well Religion,
For morals are in danger of erosion.
Bathe well Religion,
For ethics like rust are in danger of corrosion.

Disinfect well Religion,
And kill germs gestating in the embryos of disciples;
For the seeds we cultivate are in danger of decomposition,
For the seeds we plant are assaulted by microbes.

Manage well Managers,
For the people you boss will boss you tomorrow,
Supervise well supervisors,
For the seeds you nurse will nurse your own seeds.

Write well writers,
And retard the growth of invasive words.
For the strength of the pen is in the souls it tames,
For the seeds of imagination are herbs and healers.

Feed deep readers,
For the words you eat are builders and reformers,
Feed fat readers,
For the words you devour are rulers and crusaders.

Build the home woman,
For what marginalizes you advertises you.
Unlock your lips woman,
For those who criticizes you advertises you.

Use the right measurements 'Buyam Sellams',
For the scale that weights the weight of your goods,
Is the very scale that weighs the weight of your sins.

Reflections on the Social Role of Writers

Where the Pen Rules

Some say you are mightier than the sword
Some say you are greater than great Kings,
Some say you nourish more than breastmilk
The strength of the pen is in the hearts it tamed.

Some say you build more than builders
Some say you redeem more than redeemers
Some say you form more than reformers
Some say you hunt more than hunters.

Some say you rumble more than thunder
Some say you grumble more than hunger
Some say you see more than diviners
Some say you manure more than droppings.

Some say you tame more than vaccines
Some say you kill more than abortion
Some say you teach more than pedagogues.
The strength of the pen is in the storms it quenched off.

Some say you whip more than a cane
Some say you heal more than herbs
Some say you pamper more than lullabies
Some say you fight more than soldiers
While others say you sting more than bees.

So use the pen to unite,
Use the pen to vaccinate, for

In the pen I see the hunter
In the pen I see the healer
In the pen I see the Pastor
In the pen I see the activist.

※ ※

Where the Pen Heals

Buea 12th of March 2016 was the 2015 EKO Awards
In the Drama category a red feather sat quivering
In the Drama category a red feather sat quaking
Like robes of stately command a red feather was hoisted
In the drama category my academic cap was garland,
On the humble head of *The Lock on my Lips*,
On the humble head of *The Lock on my Lips*.

According to ACWA and EKO
So many ingredients went into the making of the mental menu
According to ACWA and EKO
Patriotic ingredients went into the making of the mental menu
For ACWA and EKO said
Educative ingredients went into the making of the mental meal,
For ACWA and EKO said
Self-building ingredients went into the making of the mental meal.
For ACWA and EKO said
Nutritive ingredients went into the making of the mental meal.
For ACWA and EKO what makes minds visible
Is the amount of intellectual traffic.

Buea 12th of March 2016 was the 2015 EKO Awards
The day set aside to celebrate the potency of the pen.
The day set aside for recognition of the power of the pen
The day set aside for commemoration of the virility of the pen
Which some say is mightier than the sword.

Buea 12th of March 2016 was the 2015 EKO Awards
The day set aside for commemoration of the virility of the pen
For *The Lock on my Lips* which became The Luck from my Lips,
Was the product of sperms ejaculated from imagination.

For ACWA and EKO what makes minds visible
Is the amount of intellectual traffic.

Buea 12th of March 2016 was the 2015 EKO Awards
A red feather sat quivering on the head of The Lock on my Lips,
According to EKO and ACWA
So many ingredients went into the making of the mental menu
So many ingredients went into the making of the mental meal.
From the laps of Cameroon Anglophone Academic Maternity
Sprung up *The Lock on my Lips* and other nutritious works of art;
Which Cameroon Anglophone Writers' Association
Which some call the academic spouse of ECO Foundation
Has excavated from that potent hatchery
In the race to awaken Anglophone writers from imaginative sterility
In a bid to mine the works of Cameroon Anglophone writers from
private shelfs,
And let their voices echo and reverberate beyond mountains and rivers
That separate black soil from western soil.
For ACWA and EKO what makes minds visible
Is the fertility and fecundity of the pen.

Buea 12th of March 2016 was the 2015 EKO Awards
A red feather sat on my head
A red feather sat quivering on my mental cap
A red feather sat quaking on my academic cap
A feather of recognition sat quavering on my cap
Because my mental womb has hatched a full bloom and not Which I
thought was a cripple in want of mental nurture.
For ACWA and EKO what makes minds visible
Is the amount of intellectual traffic.

Buea 12th of March 2016 was the 2015 EKO Awards
The day The Lock on my Lips was The Luck on my Lips
An evening of celebration
An evening of recognition

An evening when writers gathered
Celebrating hard work and achievements
Celebrating works of imagination
Celebrating an aspect of our culture
Celebrating the patriotic voice of Cameroon Anglophone Literature
Celebrating the pride of Cameroon Anglophone Literature,
Commemorating the collective memory of Cameroon Anglophone
heritage,
And celebrating the power of the pen
Which some say is mightier than the sword;
Celebrating the effort of EKO and Nkemngong Nkengasong,
Whose academic collaboration gave birth to EKO Price Foundation.
For ACWA and EKO what makes minds visible
Is the amount of intellectual traffic.

The Weight of Words

In words lives the children of human imagination
In words is wedged the wine of imagination
In words resides the sting of writers
In words protrude beacons of time.
In words lives the literary Empire
In words are erected muscles of muse.

In words reigns the supremacy of Imagination,
In words are lodged remnants of black heritage,
In words lives the weight of hard work
Which mental pedagogues say is harder than yard work,
In words resides the power of the pen
Which writers say is mightier than the sword.

In words lives fetters of tradition
In words resides the fury of storms,
In words are bred the anger of tyranny,
In words are propagated the tactics of terrorism.
In the very words will be conquered the terror of terrorism.

So celebrate achievements and not intensions;
Celebrate birth and not pregnancy;
Celebrate delivery and not labor and abortion;
For in words germinate seeds of love.

The strength of the writer is in the pen.
The weight of the pen is in the hatchery of its fertility clock.
The might of the pen is in the hatchery of its academic maternity.

June 2012/2016

Others

For Kongnyuy Jean Claude

Brutally nipped on the Bud,
By the pernicious and savage brute,
Why reap from my bosom my lovely bud?
You severed from the nest so unkindly
You wrenched off from the nest so untimely,
The irretrievable Treasure,
The only balm that soothes the soul,
The only balm that soothes the soul.

Insensate, impudent miscondrel
That arrives uninvited
You sever from me untimely
The irretrievable Treasure
 And on me imposes the labour
To excavate in vain what is fossilized in imagination.

O the irrecoverable Treasure
That was once so young and comforting
The one whose beauty was nowhere seen
You know I loved you dearly
Yet ingrates robbed me of You so callously.

O my handsome and beloved Jean Claude
Be Thou muffled in Thy sanctity
And never be divorced twice
If that be my prayer
Commiseration be His answer.

My immortal Treasure
Though from sight You are banished
In memory and prayer
You live with me.

1998

Patching up our Treasured-Shredding Roof

From the unfolding scene of the fury of intolerance,
When the orgy of divide veers into communal constituency,
And propaganda fuels and celebrates anthems of divide,
And progressively infects the descent from its roots to soul,
While water pipes menstruate and fart and urinate at roadsides;
Only mending and bunching and change-begins-with-me-agenda,
Will cause to abate threatening erosion of our treasure and pride.
Abort in the bud battles that slit the throats of peace and security;
Bunch around the trunk under whose foliage we are sheltered,
For dialogue is the currency with which peace is purchased,
For only in one knot will we resuscitate our treasure,
And cause to abate its recession and depression.

Like a dehydrated marriage, menopausal water pipes
Grumbling from pecking pains of crude abortion are nestled
In the warm embrace of our muscular ancestral black soils,
Feeding on assaulted urine darting out from laps of drunkards;
And in that resultant stage of protracted assault,
Blighted water pipes fart and urinate choking purr
Of stinking dark-brown slimy-muddy urine,
And now our lungs are infested and rutted and thirsty.

Breed no more volcanic breeds,
Hatch no more bigoted seeds,
Slit no more the throat of peace,
Fart no more garbage from lips,
Propagate no more explosive lures,
Sing no more in discordant tones.
Compose no more anthems of divide;
Manure no more thy tales with toxic composite,
Rouse no more motions of tempestuous alliances,

Justify no more deviancy with pathos and sentiments,
Hatch and hum melodies of grafting and mending;
Abort in the sprout volcanic lures of venomous lips.
Communicate intentions and not conclusions;
Rescind all debris that skidded off your tongues;
Make repent and atone the chorus of our ritual mantra;
And involve and listen to all rungs of the communal ladder.
Cleanse and sieve contagious propaganda of its barren debris,
Lest convulsive history reemerge and unleash its sad music.

Decontaminate all unfertile offspring of your fertile lips,
And let not the stirrings of emotion swallow reasoning.
With raffia fibre yarn from the garments of dialogue,
Patch-up our rending roof and rescue water pipes
From the fangs of weevils and locusts and termites;
For the storms that grated into shreds our umbilical roof,
Should bunch like bananas and mend the severing trunk.

Lame legs still limp from nodule blights of Yeeh and Kitiiwum;
Drought refugees and displaced refugees lodge in caves and valleys.
Save the trunk from erosion and minimize the looming damage;
Lest it crashes with us, when the throat of peace is slit again.
Like a grafted fruit, meld we into one bunch,
Repair within one voice, for only grafting in diversity,
And a sacrificial win-win-behind-the-scene whispers,
Will scuttle the propagation of chronic propaganda,
And seal the coffin of this frenzied-protracted barren epic battle.

ABOUT THE AUTHOR

Pepertua K Nkamanyang LOLA holds a PhD in Literary and Cultural Studies from Justus-Liebig University Giessen, Germany, and has lectured in several Universities in Cameroon including the Universities of Douala, Bamenda and Dschang. She has served as an editor and reviewer for the journal, *The Gong* and has published numerous articles in leading national and international journals. She is the author of the play, *The Lock on My Lips* (2014), which earned her the 2015 Eko Prize for Literature (Emerging Anglophone Writers), and *Rustles on Naked Trees (2016),* her début novel. She has worked in several administrative positions including Research and Documentation Officer (Justus Liebig University, Giessen, Germany), Deputy Mayor for Mbiame Council, Head of Service for Extra-African Cooperation (The University of Bamenda), and is currently the Cultural Attaché to the Cameroon High Commission in Abuja, Nigeria. Besides being a creative writer and critic, her teaching and core research interests are in the areas of the African Novel, Contemporary and Interdisciplinary Literary Theory and Criticism, Narratology and the narrative tradition, Postcolonial Criticism, Gender and Feminist Criticism, Cultures of Memory, and Theories of Identity.